*Changing Services*
*for Changing Clients*

# Changing Services
# for Changing Clients

*Published for the*

NATIONAL ASSOCIATION OF SOCIAL WORKERS

*by* COLUMBIA UNIVERSITY PRESS

*New York and London*

*First printing 1969*
*Second printing 1970*

Standard Book Number 0-231-03245-5
Library of Congress Catalog Card Number: 69-18878
Printed in the United States of America

# Contributors

JOHN S. MORGAN is Dean, School of Social Work, University of Pennsylvania, Philadelphia

MAURICE F. CONNERY is Associate Professor, School of Social Welfare, University of California, Los Angeles

DUANE W. BECK is Executive Director of the Community Council of the Atlanta Area, Inc., Atlanta

MYRTLE R. REUL is Associate Professor, School of Social Work, University of Georgia, Athens

NORMAN A. POLANSKY is Professor of Social Work and Sociology, School of Social Work, University of Georgia, Athens

GEORGE A. BRAGER is Associate Professor, School of Social Work, Columbia University, New York City

# *Preface*

THIS BOOK includes papers selected from regional institutes held in 1967 and sponsored by the Regional Institute Program of the National Association of Social Workers, a program activity of the Council on Social Work in Medical and Health Services within the Division of Practice and Knowledge.

The consistent theme of change, its impact on the client and the delivery of service, was of major concern to those practitioners across the country who for the 1967 institutes selected timely topics and outstanding educational directors and faculties to provide these grass-roots-based short-term educational programs.

Reference can be made to only a few of the ways in which these educational programs provided opportunity for the participants to increase their knowledge and improve their skills. Papers such as Dr. John Morgan's, presented at the Northeastern Regional Institute, add new knowledge of the major trends in the changing demands for social services. This paper, and others collected here, helped to deepen understanding about social changes and their effect on people, the social services, and the delivery of these services. Innovative demonstrations of delivery of services, an examination of the impact of new legislation on such services, the use of manpower, and related discussions stimulated the practitioners to examine critically their own practice and to be courageous and innovative in their provision of "Changing Services for Changing Clients," the topic of the 1967 Eastern Regional Institute.

It was such a challenge and the timeliness of the content that prompted the Regional Institute Program Committee to select papers related to change for publication, as well as to sponsor a unit during the NASW Second Professional Symposium on Human Services and Professional Responsibility, held in May 1968 in San Francisco.

During the past decade the Regional Institute Program has published a monograph series that has been one way to share material considered to be a valuable contribution to social work literature. This book is no exception, and it is made available by special arrangement with Columbia University Press.

Such contributions to social work literature would not be possible without the leadership and dedication of many. Sincere appreciation is expressed to those who have given so generously of their time and talents to create, and successfully produce, the 1967 institutes, and to those participants who were ready and willing to involve themselves in updating and advancing their knowledge and skills. We are appreciative also of the continued financial support of the Social Rehabilitation Services. With humility we express our pride in their continued interest and confidence in this program of continuing education for social work practitioners. Last, but not least, recognition is given to the National Association of Social Workers Board of Directors and staff, who continue to emphasize and support the important principle of continuing education for its membership.

ELEANOR J. BRADLEY
*Chairman*
*Regional Institute Program Committee*

*June 1968*
*Vancouver, B. C.*

# Contents

*Changing Services*
*for Changing Clients*

# The Changing Demand for Social Service

## JOHN S. MORGAN

WE MUST BE AWARE of the dynamic nature of the society to which we belong more in relation to trends of change than to changes that have already taken place. All around us are unsettlement, instability, and uncertainty. We must examine our own contribution to the well-being of society as a dynamic element in change, and not allow ourselves to be tethered to our preconceived ideas of what is important or useful to the people we seek to serve.

There are a number of trends for change, some of which are characteristic of North American society and some of all urban industrial societies, of which ours is today the greatest and most powerful. For purposes of this discussion, the various trends are classified under seven major headings. This will permit discussion of them in the light of social work knowledge and the standards of social well-being in a modern society, and especially examination of them in relation to what is known about people, their problems, their needs, and their capacity for change.

The history of my own family is an illustration. About the time of the Great Rebellion of 1745 in Scotland, my mother's great-great-great-grandfather was a Scottish clansman who possibly fought at the Battle of Culloden. The Scottish clans were broken up after that battle by the English Duke of Cumberland.

In the next generation, my ancestor's son was a shepherd in the Border Country of Scotland. His son became head gardener of a large estate in the southwest of Scotland, and his son became a farmworker in the rural county of Yorkshire. His son migrated to the steel town of Sheffield in the south of Yorkshire at the end of the last century and started a small business as a steel file manufacturer. This small steel manufacturer was my maternal grandfather. My mother married a steel master who was manager of one of the steel mills during the period of Great Britain's greatest industrial productivity, between 1900 and 1925. All of his children became members of the professions. Here is encapsulated the whole history of the earlier Industrial Revolution.

It has taken this family seven generations to make these social, industrial, educational, and personal adaptations. We are now expecting people in underdeveloped countries, and indeed many of our own people in this country, to make these enormous social, industrial, educational, and community changes not in seven generations, not even within one lifetime, but within a short period of perhaps one-third of a lifetime. The strains and stresses of this enormous and rapid adaptation of human life to the conditions of a modern industrial society are among the major sources of our contemporary social dysfunctions and disorders. The things about which we are all so worried, the breakdown of the family, the increase in mental illness, the alienation in our great cities, the growing instability of young people in our modern society, are not in themselves the diseases, but are the symptoms arising from rapid and only partially assimilated changes in the human condition required of all of us in this uncertain age.

*Major Trends in Service Demands*

The seven major trends in the changing demands for social services which I detect in our own country and throughout the world are as follows:

1. From curative to preventive services.

2. From individualized to universalized services and, in this connection, from small-scale to large-scale operations.

3. From private to public responsibility for the social services.

4. From services providing income only to services that provide income with additional service benefits.

5. From the criterion of poverty to the criterion of need as a test of eligibility for social services.

6. From a treatment orientation of services to the social administration of large-scale services.

7. From a limited view of welfare as a palliative based on current assumptions about the distribution of wealth or about personal responsibility for well-being to a broader view of welfare as encompassing the human condition.

Each of these headings will now be discussed in relation to the current scene.

*From cure to prevention.* These words occur often in discussion of every sphere of social services, at least among those discussing the expansion of social services. A model exists in the public health services that developed in the late nineteenth and early twentieth centuries as an extension of the curative medical services. Unfortunately, there is as yet no science of social etiology. We are much less certain than we need to be

about the underlying conditions to which we should address
ourselves in considering the whole concept of prevention.    In
the report of the Advisory Council on Public Welfare, *Having
the Power, We Have the Duty,* [1] the following statement occurs:

The lack of social services for families, young people and individuals
isolated by age and disability is itself a major factor in the perpetua-
tion of such social evils as crime and juvenile delinquency, mental
illness, illegitimacy, multi-generational dependencies, slum environment and the widely deplored climate of unrest, alienation and discouragement among many groups in the population.

This statement is vague and unsatisfactory.    There is little hard
evidence that lack of social services (what services?) is the
cause of crime or of mental illness.    The most that could be
said is that the lack of some specific services—for example,
probation services or mental health clinics—makes it difficult to
deal with some of the already evident and existing human needs
exhibited in the form of criminal behavior or mental disorder.

If we are going to talk about preventive services with any real
hope of establishing them genuinely, we must know a great deal
more about the underlying causes of the conditions that are
symptomatic of the disorders that so much distress us.

We are clearly aware of the preventive nature of a good
income maintenance system.    In a cash-based society an adequate income prevents many forms of social deprivation.    To
use the classification of Lord (then Sir) William Beveridge in
his famous report of the 1940s, we must think of adequate cash
income for a family as being a major preventive of squalor, of
malnutrition, of ignorance, and of generally unsatisfactory living conditions.    The question we need to ask ourselves is "Do
we see income maintenance as having this function, or are we
hampered by concepts such as the moral value of work for

[1] U. S. Advisory Council on Public Welfare, *Having the Power, We
Have the Duty,* Washington, D. C., U. S. Government Printing Office
(June 1966).

wages?" In other words, do we think it is more important that people work for an inadequate wage rather than receive a sufficient income as part of the appropriate distribution of the enormous wealth-producing capacity of modern industrial society? The evidence is that we do not see our income maintenance services as having a preventive function of this kind. We only have to look at the low levels of public assistance benefits in this country or in England, where the now familiar "wage-stop" limits the rates of public assistance so that the individual and his family are not to receive in benefits more than the wage the breadwinner received when employed. This nineteenth-century economic moralism raises some very real questions about the objectives of our income maintenance programs.

Take this country's programs of housing, health, rehabilitation, and indeed the whole range of social services. Are these seen as repair jobs for existing visible needs or as genuinely preventive, that is to say, as genuinely intended to prevent the emergence of conditions that are now believed to be preventable? How are we to know what service prevents which unsatisfactory human condition?

Prevention must be thought of much more as the public health specialists have come to see the public health services, namely, as services that are relevant for whole populations. Social need is a normal human phenomenon. All of us have a variety of needs at various times in the cycle of growth and family life. All of us have needs for help of one kind or another, and all of us must, in modern times, look to the society to which we belong to provide the kinds of services that will enable us to function adequately and satisfactorily in our complex urban industrial world. All of us have a need for clean air and water and measures concerned with air and water pollution must be services for all, not just some, people.

This fact became startlingly clear about two years ago at a

seminar for senior public welfare officials in Canada, practical and hard-headed representatives of the public and private services, all of them holding responsible positions and many of them professional people with long experience in the development and maintenance of social services of various kinds. It was interesting to observe that after discussing the real nature of preventive services, all present spoke as if the social services were relevant to and should be provided for the whole population, on the assumption that prevention requires us to think not so much of people who have been hurt, but to create conditions in which people whom we do not know and cannot identify will not in fact be hurt or show symptoms of social disorder.

This fact, however, must not blind us to the needs that are not visible for large sections of the population. The government of the United States, in a 1965 publication entitled "The Dimensions of Poverty," set out some figures showing that in 1964 a total population of 189,900,000 included 34,000,000 who could clearly be defined as living in poverty. Of these, only 7,400,000 were receiving public assistance. Poverty is therefore not a welfare problem but an economic problem of industrial society. It can only be tackled preventively by tackling the causes of poverty, by re-examining the whole of our arrangements for the distribution of the abundant wealth our technological society is now capable of producing. In the meantime, social security and public assistance must mitigate the present consequences of existing poverty; but they can never be cures for poverty and they can never be essentially preventives of conditions of poverty.

The discussion of social services as preventive rather than curative requires us to think about them in at least three new dimensions. First, we must find a new way of thinking about the social services themselves and their application to society.

Second, we must make a more rigorous inquiry into the causes of social illness.    Third, we must have a more generalized concept of the constituency of welfare or social services as they are applied to the over-all preventive needs affecting whole populations.

*From individualized to universalized services.*    Attention is often drawn to the fact that modern social services have developed largely from the private agencies of the past fifty years, and in particular have relied on the contribution of psychological insights into individual needs.    But as the figures in relation to poverty show, and as the growing needs of the aged are brought to our attention, it becomes clear that the modern social needs affect large populations.    This immediately raises the question of the extent to which and the ways in which the knowledge and methods of the social services as we know them (in particular, professional social work services as many of us learned them at school) can be adapted to the more universal needs of these greatly expanded client groups.

One area in which universality is being generally accepted is in relation to income maintenance.    Here the emergence of the notion of a guaranteed minimum income, to quote only one example, indicates that we are beginning to recognize the importance of an income provision that is valid for the whole population, whether or not they are able to extract that income from their daily work.    Another example of a universalized benefit that has been adopted in every industrial country in the world, except the United States, is a program of family allowances or universal children's allowances.[2]    The growing pattern of basic old-age benefits for all residents, notably in Sweden and more

[2] Eveline M. Burns, ed., *Family Allowances and the Economic Well-Being of Children,* New York: Citizens' Committee for Children (1968).

recently in Canada, with a wage-related supplementary benefit, is a further indication of the extension of universalized income maintenance schemes.

It is also important to notice the widespread reaction in all industrialized societies. This can be seen in the unwillingness of Congress to press ahead with the antipoverty legislation and in the restrictions it has placed on Aid to Families with Dependent Children in the 1967 Amendments to the Social Security Act. In France the social security "reforms" announced in 1967 by President de Gaulle and his Cabinet are clearly intended to reduce the benefits and increase the contributions made by industrial workers at a time when the cost of living is rising rapidly.

This is a reaction of which we must be aware, in that it reflects the growing reluctance among the majority of people for whom the present industrial society provides a relatively good living to sacrifice any part of their own affluence for the benefit of those who have not been able to take advantage of the technological changes and the increased affluence.

In the light of this wave of negative reaction, we shall have to consider our responsibility as social workers for promoting a continued understanding that there is still a large section of society that has not been able to take advantage of modern industrial improvements and raise its standards of living even to what any of us would regard as an adequate level.

As one examines the implications of this trend from individualized to universalized services, the need for the development of the art and practice of social administration is apparent. This is in fact one of the outstnding findings of the recent United Nations reappraisal of its technical assistance programs.

What new areas of social science knowledge must be opened to improve administration? It is essential that we draw on fundamental knowledge of organization theory, systems theory, communication theory, small group theory, and modern developments in personality theory.

We must examine some of the problems of incentives and rewards in society. It is clearly no longer sufficient to look only at the monetary rewards of a proper contribution to industrial production or to social well-being. We must also look at what people expect for rewards in the form of improved status, increased power, and a sense of achievement. But this alone will not be sufficient to provide us with an adequate base for social administration. We must also find forms of administration that are infused and shot through with the human values and with the value system that are fundamental to the practice of social work. The objectives we seek to achieve are social objectives and they will be achieved only if the persons responsible for administration hold those values themselves and work with people in ways that are not antagonistic to the end purposes they seek to achieve. Here lies the challenge to social work for the expansion and development of its notions of practice to include the practice of social administration as a method of social work.

*From private to public responsibility.* It is not surprising that there is a serious shortage of resources, manpower, teachers, money, buildings, and other essential requirements for good social services. The sheer scale of both needs and services as they affect whole nations and communities means that priorities must be established. The priority of being able to pay for service is no longer morally acceptable. This means that

priority decisions must be made on the basis of public policy—
that is to say, if a nation lacks sufficient dentists to provide
adequate dental care for a whole population, some decision
must be made about who is to receive the available dental resources.   Some countries, such as Canada or Great Britain,
have made the decision to provide adequate services for children on the sound principle that it is better to devote available
dental resources to the preservation of the teeth of the next
generation than to expand the provision of massive dental care
for those whose teeth have already begun to show serious deterioration.

It is this need to establish priorities in the public interest, as
much as the need to mobilize massive resources, that leads us to
turn to the public services as the basic resource for the new
types of social service that are emerging in various industrial
countries.   This in turn raises new problems in the allocation of
scarce resources.   Foreign policy, industrial production, agricultural policy are all now to be taken into account in the
allocation of the total resources of the nation.   The social services have to be seen in the context of the total national economy, and decisions have to be made about the proportion of the
national income and skilled manpower that can be devoted at
any given time to the prevention of social disorder and to the
repair and easement of social conditions that have already
arisen and that in the judgment of the community must be
alleviated or cured.

Another new criterion arises in relation to the provision of
public services, the whole area of acccountability.   For example, when a professional person, such as a doctor, psychiatrist, or dentist, is in private practice, the only persons to
whom he is accountable are his clients and, in respect to his
professional behavior, to his profession.   But when dental or

mental health care is made a public provision, the provider of service must now be accountable to the community as a whole for the way in which he uses their resources.[3]

This question is preliminary to consideration of the place of the private agency in the modern social service complex. The discussion so far poses the problem of relevance. Needs—human needs—are as varied as humanity. The private agency is a selective instrument, and it must now move into new areas uncovered by the establishment of universal public services. That is, as gross poverty becomes essentially a public responsibility, specific types of poverty will be uncovered that cannot be dealt with on the basis of averages or by some general public service. This is an unexplored area in which the private agencies have a responsibility to examine their place as the explorers and forerunners of new services, and as the responsible agents of society, in taking care of the special areas that have now been uncovered. In the field of health, the major killer diseases have successfully been brought under control through public health care, by immunization, and by the rapid development of modern medical sciences. So we have uncovered the more hidden health needs, and particularly the social and mental health needs, that could not be given attention so long as massive epidemics had to be dealt with.

The development of new social services on a selective basis, to meet newly uncovered needs, will require a high degree of individualization and selectivity. These seem to be two characteristics of the private agency field that open the way to new and

[3] This is only one aspect of the whole problem of social accounting to which Bertram Gross has given prominence in his recent writings, particularly in his Social Science Paperback entitled *The State of the Nation* where he examines some of the many difficult problems of social systems accounting. See Bertram M. Gross, *The State of the Nation,* London: Social Science Paperbacks (1966).

exciting adventures in the development of social services. It does, however, pose for the profession a number of very real problems. It will involve us in re-examining much of our present practice and many of our present assumptions about the nature and character of services. It also imposes on the practitioner the responsibility for identifying and exploring, first on a research basis, the frontiers of the existing and expanding services in order to see where these new needs really are and what services are needed to meet them.

*From income alone to income plus services.* It is evident from the legislation that is now proceeding through the legislatures of various countries that it has been recognized that the provision of an income, while essential in itself, does not in fact enable many people to receive basic needed services. The 1962 Amendments to the Social Security Act with their emphasis on services, or Titles XVIII and XIX, added in 1967, which provide Medicare and Medicaid, illustrate this point.

Most of these services require public action, because they call for the mobilization of services in a degree and a quantity that simply cannot be achieved by the individual. Nor indeed can the private agencies, out of their own resources, mobilize anything like the volume, variety, or quality of services that many of their clients need.

In a pluralistic society such as ours, it is both reasonable and desirable that there should be more than one provider of service. Indeed, there is so much to be done that there should be more concern with underlapping and inadequate coordination than with any question of duplication. The private agencies are the guarantors of this essential pluralism. There is, however, a real need for private agencies to concentrate on the provision of new services as the public sector increasingly absorbs the mass programs.

*From poverty to need.* It is no longer morally acceptable to social work as a profession that social services be provided only to those who are poor. There is, however, a marked reaction in many parts of the world, where considerable effort is being made to return to the means test for receipt of services.

However, if poverty is removed as a criterion, it must be replaced by some other test of eligibility. We have to search for adequate and administratively feasible tests of eligibility for service, for example, in relation to public housing, special education, and medical care of all kinds. So far, no satisfactory criterion has been found. The recent developments under Title XIX of the Social Security Act do in fact make an economic test, the test of eligibility for medical care. The fact that some states, such as New York, have a generous test and that other states are likely to have a much less generous one, indicates the undesirability and unreliability of an economic test of need in relation to the need for medical care. There has to be a test of need, and if it is not to be a financial test, what is it to be and how is it to be administered? Here again is a problem of creating *social* administration, not financial or political administration, but administration that achieves social objectives by social means. It is clear that if we are to move from making poverty the main ground for the provision of social services to some other criterion we have yet a long way to go in developing adequate, socially justifiable, and administratively feasible tests in order to establish the eligibility for a service. The trend now visible in the public welfare field, to separate income maintenance from service benefits, is an indication that we are aware of the problem, but there is little evidence that we have yet tackled the other subsequent problem of achieving socially just and administratively feasible ways of testing the eligibility of clients for service. The current battle in Britain is on this very point—a struggle between "selectivity" (that is, tested need for service) and universal service. The result of this debate may affect all of us in the near future.

*From treatment to social administration.*  This does not mean, and should not mean, that treatment services will be diminished, but that new large-scale universalized service will be added in order to make available to people services that they can use if they need them, and without any consideration of a specific treatment orientation.  We need to examine carefully the proposition that treatment means professional takeover of the responsibility for diagnosis and care of the problem, whereas with the newer universalized services the client retains responsibility for seeking and using the service.  For example, the homemaker service is rapidly developing on this continent, and in another form is a municipal social service in Great Britain of great importance to both the social and medical services of that country.  Here the need is for the provision of a reliable and satisfactory homemaker service that the client can obtain when he decides that he needs this additional support for the maintenance of his home and family life.

If these services are to be successful, the client must be an essential partner in the administrative process.  This will require social work practice of a high order but with a new orientation.  In order to achieve it, it will be necessary to undertake painstaking research and bold experimentation, based on the primary assumptions that the selection of the service is the responsibility of the client and that the use to be made of the service is primarily a matter for the client's own decision.

*From a limited to a broad view of welfare.*  This raises a new array of problems.  First among these are the problems of the corporate responsibility of the community as a whole and the problem of the citizen's individual responsibility. The essential problem here is to design social service operations that retain the essential responsibility of the client and make the service available to a person of a kind, of a quality, and in a quantity that are relevant to his need. Perhaps the best example of this new range of problems is to be found in the field of urban redevelopment and public housing. Here again, one of the major issues is that of the nature and quality of the administration of the social services. The social and biological sciences must provide additional knowledge but social work must provide know-how, and the know-how must now include the deployment of resources in large-scale operations with adequately trained staff. The aim must not be a welfare state with passive recipients of bounty whether from public or private agencies, but a socially responsible state in which the citizen is able to take an active part in creating and operating as well as in using some services appropriately and effectively. As Lord Beveridge once said, "The happiness or unhappiness of the society in which we live depends on ourselves as individuals."

*Problems for the Profession*

This brief analysis of the changes that can be detected in the direction and pattern of development in the social services raises a number of major problems for social work and the social work profession. There are a number of these implications of major importance.

First, more emphasis must be given to the identification of social need in addition to and perhaps in place of the diagnosis of individual need.[4]

[4] See, for example, Frances Fox Piven and Richard A. Cloward, "Desegregated Housing: Who Pays for the Reformer's Ideal?" in *The New Republic,* December 1966.

Second, concentration must be placed on identification of the social components of large-scale welfare or social service operations. It must be recognized that many of the social welfare programs that are now needed to deal with the social consequences of the industrial and technological revolution are services requiring a great many professional disciplines, including housing and town planning, urban redevelopment, new patterns of education, new patterns of recreation, and many others.

The need here is to identify those parts of the total program to which the values of social work and the skills of social work practice have a unique and significant contribution to make. Unless these kinds of identifications are made, the probability is that the plans will go ahead without the kinds of values, social objectives, or patterns of administration and management that ought to be brought in by social workers with their knowledge of human behavior, their value structure of respect for human dignity, and capacity to recognize the fundamental elements of human need.

Third, a real problem for social work will be identification of the social aspects of economic and political programs. All of these, on superficial examination, seem to be questions mainly for the economist. It is only when one examines the impact of any one of these programs on the lives and habits of individuals and families at all levels of the social spectrum that one realizes the immense power for good or evil in the lives of people of schemes for the management of the national economy and the introduction of massive public programs with implications for the redistribution of the national income.

Fourth, the need for the expansion of our concept of "professional practice" as a new era of concern for the social work profession must be studied. On the one hand, the concept of professional practice must be expanded (as suggested earlier) to the urgent necessity for the development of an art and skill of social administration.   We must examine the need also for other new forms of practice, such as those to which attention is drawn in the papers recently published by the Council on Social Work Education [5] on the antipoverty programs and the implications of these programs for personnel.   These papers draw specific attention to many areas of practice.   Dr. Simon Slavin of the Columbia University School of Social Work draws attention to the need for the practice of "skill in social policy analysis formulation, development and evaluation."   He points out that while at present we tend to think of social policy and services as the essential background information about setting for the practice of social work, in his view they have now become "for many social workers, operational—a form of social work practice, a 'doing' as well as 'knowing.' "

This leads at once to the fifth major problem, the redefinition and alignment of the main directions of social work education.   This does not mean discarding what we now have.   On the contrary, it means enriching and enlarging what we now have to incorporate both the insights of knowledge and the understandings of practice in new types of professional activity aimed at the new needs that have been uncovered by the situations with which we are now faced and by the new kinds of diagnosis of social need to which attention has already been drawn.

Our efforts to contribute a responsible professional reaction to any major trends in change of demand, and many of the problems for the profession, will depend for usefulness and development on a considerable expansion of research.   It is also

[5] Barr, Normandia, Piven, Schurr, Stea, and Slavin, *Personnel in Anti-Poverty Programs: Implications for Social Work Education,* New York: Council on Social Work Education (1967).

true that one of the kinds of research to which a great deal more attention should be devoted is comparative study of situations in different types of communities and in different nations. We will possibly understand better what the essentials of practice are if we can see the practice at work within the very different cultural and social assumptions of other communities and other countries.

Sixth, but by no means last, we must also begin to examine the implications for the profession of social work as the skilled art and practice of encouraging and developing community change. This in a way may well be a return to the traditions of people like Jane Addams and many others who devoted their professional lives to changing not only the societies in which they then lived, but also to changing the institutions of social organization and community service provision. The difference will be that our task, in some ways more exciting, and in some ways more difficult, will require us to involve the clients in the development not only of changes, but also in the diagnosis of the problem and in the directions in which developments for its assimilation must be sought.

## Challenges to Professional Thought

All of these trends and problems raise a number of challenges to our whole pattern of professional thought. In areas in which we are particularly challenged we must examine and reexamine our corporate thinking as a profession, as well as our whole patterns of thought as individual members of the profession.

It is often said but far too often not accepted or fully understood that we now recognize poverty, ill health, unemployment, old age, vocational disability, and many other forms of human disablement as not in fact either the responsibility of the individual or capable of being dealt with by individual action of the persons most concerned. The difficulty here is not only to persuade ourselves and the community to accept these as community responsibilities, but also to find out how to undertake services for people to meet these kinds of needs, and yet at the same time retain for the individual client a real and genuine responsibility in his approach to and use of public services. There is a real danger that in our anxiety to make services available we shall so organize and administer them that they will be, so to speak, provided by the "anonymous state," and that this may quite easily lead the ordinary citizen to regard the state as "fair game" for anything that can be obtained. In so doing, the probability is that the value of the services to him will be markedly diminished if not totally destroyed. This is one of the many problems in the analysis of human behavior that the social work profession ought to examine.

The second group of challenges is of a more fundamental kind. It will probably be quite impossible to make any serious inroads on the appalling housing situation in the large industrial cities if we are compelled by the social attitudes of society to be as respectful as we have hitherto been to the rights of private property. In the same way, in the development of services, escially those services that involve the use of scarce resources such as medical care, we are unlikely to make any substantial progress so long as we are as respectful as we have hitherto been of the overriding values of private enterprise.

Similarly, we have too easily accepted the view that work is itself a good thing, and that money obtained from employment (which we call wages) has in itself an inherent social value. This is a relatively recent idea in the long-range view of human affairs. The rapid change in the productive capacity of machines raises questions about our whole assumption of the moral value of "work" and "wages."

In the cybernated factory where the machine, whose production- and tending-cost stands in little relation to its ability to produce goods, is the main source of wealth, how can the workers' worth be evaluated in production units?   When the amount of the human muscle expended in making an item was an essential element of its value, both the muscle and the product could be computed in terms of labor time (the wages of the muscle and the product).   But if that is no longer the case, how can income, the right to consume, be tied to a labor time that is less and less relevant? [6]

Here we are likely to find most serious resistance to change, not only among the political conservatives but also especially among captains of industry and leaders of organized labor, whose whole traditions have been based on the supremacy of work as a value and the virtue of wages as an incentive.

Last, but by no means least, is the age-old question of class structure and class status.   One of the underlying discontents of most of our city societies today is obviously the citizen appre- hension arising from lack of social, economic, and political power in situations that profoundly affect their whole way of living.

Until we are prepared to examine objectively, and without predetermination of our conclusions, some of these sacred assumptions, we are unlikely to make any serious or effective approaches to many of our problems such as housing, medical care, income maintenance, or indeed begin to comprehend the social needs of the alienated societies of our inner cities.   These are not problems to be solved by statistical analysis, although statistical analysis may well tell us where and when the judg-

[6] Michael Harrington, *The Accidental Century,* New York: The Mac- millan Co. (1965).

nents required of us will be relevant and our decisions will be effective. In the last analysis, they are questions of good and evil in the whole context of human values in our society and in our neighbor societies throughout the world as we now know it. It is this interrelation of social, political, and economic policies within a moral framework that sets the stage for the kind of reexamination that is needed.

A single quotation for our guidance might well be a dictum of Pestalozzi's: [7] "Wir wollen nicht die Verstaadt lichung der Menschen sondern die Vermenschilichung des Staates"—"What is needed is not the nationalization of the human being, but the humanizing of the nation."

[7] John Huddelston, "Socialism in the Societies," *Contemporary Review,* July 1967, p. 2.

# Changing Services
# for Changing Clients

## MAURICE F. CONNERY

IN ALL GREAT RELIGIONS of the world, there is a time set apar
when believers are called to pause and, individually and collec
tively, to look backward as well as forward before the nex
stage in the journey is begun. It is a time to look inward a
well as outward—to slough off the impedimenta that have en
cumbered us, to mobilize our resources, and to chart the cours
of the next ascent. Each of us in his own small way realize
that man is poised at a critical phase in his development durin
which it shall be decided whether he and the society he ha
fashioned shall disappear, another of the innumerable, unsuccess
ful experiments of evolution, or whether he shall burst the con
straints that bind him to the mud from which he arose and begi
to realize more fully the vision he dimly perceives.

### Relevance and Identity of Social Work

To some it may seem extravagance or empty hyperbole to
speak of social work and social casework in this context
There was a time when the nation little noted nor long remem
bered the doings of social workers. During that period ou
meetings often featured learned discourses on the relative excel
lence of a newly isolated defense mechanism or the presentatio

of briefs concerning whether or not the friendly home visitor should accept the client's offer of a cup of coffee. For a long time social work was a backwater of our society, relatively sealed off from the mainstream of our national concerns. Those days are over. Today what we say, what we believe, and what we do are taken seriously, for the issues that have been our traditional concern have become among the most critical of our time.

But to be listened to, to be taken seriously, does not guarantee that we shall have any influence. Ours is a skeptical, pragmatic age, more responsive to deeds than to designs, to facts than to philosophies. There is little question that the issues of social welfare have moved into the center stage of our national and international concerns. Whether or not social work will be a significant voice in this drama, whether or not we shall be assigned a significant role in the decisions to be taken, is still moot. It is in this perspective of a search to establish our relevance to the great issues and demands of our time that we must interpret the ferment that is now taking place in all of social work.

The defense of social welfare's relevance, however, has been misdirected and narrowly construed. Too often the identity of social work has been linked to a specific problem or a particular population. Whether the problems to which we have traditionally addressed ourselves or the populations with whom we have been most intimately engaged shall continue to demand our attention in the foreseeable future is not the issue. Our future is no more dependent on whether or not there will be public assistance recipients, unmarried mothers, or the mentally ill than the future of medicine is dependent on the persistence of any specific disease. These are but epiphenomena of a process that in one form or other shall be with us for a long time, if not

forever, for challenge and change, stress and crisis are not anti
thetical to life but are of its essence.

Neither is the identity of social work irrevocably imbedded in
any specific structure or fixed methodology. Contrary to
the American Medical Association, medicine is medicine
whether it is practiced within the socialized framework of Soviet
society no less than within our own free enterprise system
whether its instruments are a surgeon's scalpel or a laser beam
The same is true of social work.  Institutions, professions
methodologies, like any phenomena of life, must evolve, de
velop, or perish.  Unlike some organisms, social work did not
come into existence preprogrammed.  The task of social work
is to seek, within the degrees of freedom that have been given to
it, to influence the direction of this evolution.

### Social Work As a Social Institution

It would be comforting to unveil a grand design that would
fulfill those great expectations necessary to our task.  Such is
not possible, but within the general perspective it is possible for
us meaningfully to reexamine where we have been, where we
now are, what we are doing, and what choices confront us in the
immediate future.  Let us begin to examine what these senti-
ments have to do with social work and social casework in particular.  Let us look at how we have formulated the mission
of social work in American society, and how this formulation
has influenced the direction of our professional development.

Social work as a social institution and as a profession came
into existence when it was somewhat reluctantly accepted that
the problems of the poor and disadvantaged were not transitory
phenomena to be swept away by the inevitable tide of progress,
or that money, birth, or social status were sufficient prophylaxis

against the stresses of a complex society. If faith in an inevitable progress failed us, science and American organizational know-how stood ready to fill the vacuum. Oversimply stated, this thinking went as follows: Every problem, individual or social, was perceived as a puzzle for which there existed a solution. The execution of this solution required an expertise, preferably based on some scientific discipline. Society therefore delegates to selected disciplines and institutions responsibility for the management of the problems that are its concern, and fosters the growth and development of these institutions and professions by providing the support and reward commensurate with their efforts. Thus reassured, the community goes about the processes of living, absolved from any further responsibility with respect to these problems. One might characterize the era that developed as the product of this thinking as the age of the professional. The emergence or identification of a new problem was quickly followed by the development of a new profession.

The initial success of this covenant is evident in both medicine and engineering. Once demonic possession was no longer a tenable explanation for mental illness and it was redefined as a medical problem, the management of this problem was turned over to psychiatrists who obligingly accepted the assignment with every assurance that they were equal to the task. Equally confident were the educators in accepting the responsibility for preparing our youths for entering a technological society. Social work was also a part of this process. The experience of the Civil War had stilled those voices that had begun to question the fundamental premises upon which our emerging society was predicated, and had given Americans a new confidence in the applicability of the principles of science and industrial organization to the problems of social welfare. It was an era that saw the emergence of bureaucratized social welfare institutions, the professional social worker, and a growing distrust of the amateur.  Thus social work confidently accepted the responsibility to solve the problems of the poor and otherwise socially disadvantaged, and committed itself to the development of a structure and method by which this assignment could be carried out. There were but a few voices raised to question this contract, to ask whether our assignment was truly one that could be fulfilled without changing the basic premises of our society, whether it was wise or possible to absolve the community of obligations other than fiscal.

For a time it looked as though the contract might be satisfactory for all concerned.  Medicine regularly produced its quota of magic bullets, and with equal regularity engineers fashioned machines and devices sufficient to satisfy our technological appetites.  Social welfare was less spectacularly successful, but periodically social workers too brought forth a new therapy or invention promising that soon all would be well.

The immediate result of this development was a schism within our society that separated the professional community from the lay community, and indeed the professionals from one another.  There emerged that limbo world of the untrained social worker, and superordinate to the whole system, the theorist from whom flowed all that was good and true.  This society has been dubbed by some as the credential society within which one's movement is narrowly determined.  A less obvious, but perhaps in the long run a more lasting consequence of this development, was a withdrawal from direct and active concern with the problems of social welfare by those very groups and individuals whose participation was essential to its vitality. Not the least of these was the exclusion of the client population itself.  The structure and conceptualization of social work practice that derived from these premises inevitably reflected a greater concern with structure and process than with ideology. We fashioned a model of service whose deficiencies we could mask by contending that it was just a matter of getting a greater supply of professional workers to commit themselves to a rarely questioned structure and process.

## Increasing Specialization of Social Work

Decades ago Darwin demonstrated that no species survives or flourishes in isolation from meaningful transaction with its many environments. Social work in general and social casework in particular have suffered from their failure to evolve a practice that is predicated on these necessary linkages. We are distressed when client groups demand a part in the dialogue on how their problems shall be met, by whom, and where. We have been equally awkward in our use of volunteers and indigenous associates, sometimes finding it harder to accept their successes than their failures. Some sage has remarked that war is too important to be left to the military. Now that the concerns of social work have been escalated to issues of critical national and international import, the same may rightfully be said of social welfare. We can no longer claim so vast a territorial exclusivity.

This is not new. What may be less obvious, but equally important, is our awareness of the degree to which our structures and patterns for the organization and delivery of social services has been conditioned by, and continues to reflect, this narrowed perspective. Less fully recognized, perhaps, is that if we are to ensure our continued relevance as a social institution we must create both structures and practice strategies that are compatible with the community's fullest engagement in our efforts. Invaluable experience was gained from innovations in the organization and delivery of social services that have come about in programs sponsored by the Office of Economic Opportunity.

Parallel to these developments has been the aggressive entry into what was once the more or less exclusive purview of social workers of a whole new array of professional persons whose styles and orientations are unfamiliar to us. The lawyer, the experimental psychologist, and the systems analyst have discovered that there is a greater challenge in charting a successful path through the welfare bureaucracy than in programming a rocket course to the moon. At times we may wish nostalgically for the halcyon days when the only intruder in our act was the friendly psychoanalyst. However, practice developments that ignore the new realities are doomed to the inconsequence of a rose petal falling in the Grand Canyon. On the other hand, the potential of the orchestration of these many new voices stirs our imagination. Although there is no single shining illustration that clearly demonstrates this potential, we do have fragmentary reports of neighborhood service centers, some of the work of the Mobilization For Youth program in New York, Elliot Studt's work in the California penal system, and other developments that suggest the emergence of new strategies of practice within which social workers, while not always center stage, have established their relevance and made their presence felt.

## Social Work in the Marketplace

If the pace of this renovation of social work practice is to be quickened, we must strip away some of the encumbering mystique that has impeded our treatment efforts. Casework treatment in this context becomes not something esoteric but rather a human encounter that springs from the universal striving of all men to achieve self-realization in a human society. Casework students often fret with the realization that often the grand and elegant designs spun for the benefit of the client are constantly frustrated by the client's perverse attention to other voices, or the intrusion of influences in his life not included in the "script." He envies the psychoanalyst who demands withdrawal of his client from the madding crowd, the suspension of time and reality, and the postponement of commitment and decision. Whatever the dreams of social workers, events have dragged us, albeit reluctantly, out of our quiet bowers into the marketplace. For better or for worse this is our place, noisy and unneat though it may be. And it is within this environment that we must find our place and the means of establishing our relevance. There is a vitality in the marketplace, and the last decade has witnessed great advances in social work practice that have been achieved as we have become more comfortable with this environment. It is true that we are finding it harder and harder to identify those clients whose metamorphosis is so clearly the exclusive product of our effort. More often what we do melds imperceptibly into the larger tides and the sometimes pedestrian activities of the community where ultimately life is lived and problems solved. Our helping methodologies have not yet fully reflected our location in the marketplace or our full engagement in the life of the community. Yet there have been significant advances which suggest that we are on the right track. We are discovering that one may have a problem without being one, that insight may be the product of action as truly as of contemplation, and finally, that we have only begun to understand the many-faceted mysteries of the human potential. Examples of significant evolutions in our concepts of treatment and practice include the exciting advances in crisis theory and practice, the creative innovations in the use of family agents working in conjunction with the professional social worker, new patterns in the organization and delivery of service to the aged and chronically ill, and the creative engagement of social workers in all phases of the many new community mental health programs. What distinguishes all these efforts is a refreshing humility with respect to our capabilities, a fidelity to the mission of social work, and a more effective understanding of engagement with other forces in the community.

## *Need for a Changing Structure of Social Work*

As we have begun to re-examine the processes of social work, our attention has been directed inevitably to the structures through which social work services and social casework services in particular are provided. It is not surprising that the structure of social work practice has changed little in an era characterized by change. Some have likened the structures of social work practice to a Maginot Line defense in an era of mobile warfare. Whatever the validity of this metaphor, it becomes daily more clear that a gap exists between our current conceptions of the nature of the tasks of social welfare, the necessary and sufficient conditions of social work practice, and the organization and procedures designed for its execution. Obstetricians have been somewhat less than completely successful in assuring that all babies present themselves for delivery between nine and five, Monday through Friday, holidays and vacation periods excepted. Yet if one were to judge from the structure and organization of social work practice, problems come neatly labeled, and for every madness there exists an appropriate method. If social work is to establish relevance in meeting the stress and crises of daily living something has to give in the calendars of social agencies and in the monogamy of the casework relationship. The clients can make the necessary adjustments, but the outcome of the drama for traditionally trained social workers is less certain. Necessity and reality are the parents of invention, and there are many exciting new developments in the organization of practice that invite our attention. Among these is the work of Elliot Studt. She describes the organization of fluid task teams through which our total resources can be realized maximally. Comparable developments have been reported by the Los Angeles Suicide Prevention Center and in the work of the Family Crisis Program at the Colorado Medical School, directed by Dr. David Kaplan. What all these efforts share is a readiness to create strategies of helping and to adapt structures that will conform to the realities of people in trouble rather than to the demands of professional convenience or tradition. If we are to take our place in the marketplace we must fashion a design for action that befits the conditions of the marketplace. As McLuhan reminds us, the medium is the message.

## The Problem-Area Approach

Despite the caveats raised about the dangers of an exaggerated professionalism, if social workers are to resolve effectively the complex problems of social welfare, they are going to be more rather than less necessary. We are only beginning to appreciate the wide range of skills, knowledge, attitudes, and experience necessary to meet the complex demands of social welfare problems. Some of these competences are widely distributed in the community. Others are the product of engagement in related activities. Some are quickly acquired through engagement in the helping process, but others can be realized only through exacting study and rigid discipline. There is much in effective social work practice that is applied common sense. There is also much that violates its canons. There is much in the necessary knowledge base of social work practice that is not the by-product of the average or even unusual life experience. There is much in the practice of social work that is "unnatural," which for its execution requires training and supportive structures that make possible the continued commitment to what is often a lonely road.

In our determination to escape the constraints of parochial professionalism and to re-establish the continuities between the helping processes of social work and the larger processes of human endeavor, we have quite properly emphasized the differences that bind together the many components of the community. But to assume that equality requires the negation of difference or to deny real differences when such exist is an act of serious irresponsibility. Thus, while most of us would subscribe to the idea that the achievement of physical health is a quest in which others than the physician must play an active role, it is doubtful whether any of us would submit to surgery by an individual who had not graduated from an accredited medical school, or whose competence had not been certified by some responsible board. Comparable competences are necessary to the successful execution of social welfare practice. Unfortunately, social work competences are not so easily identified. It is, nevertheless, a task to which we must commit ourselves.

Part of the difficulty that has beset social work as it moves toward the specification of its competences has originated with some exaggeratedly grandiose expectations of the level and range of competence that can realistically be encompassed by the average social worker at any one time or in any one place. The idea that the professional social worker is an interchangeable part who can be moved from one area of practice to another, or even operate within the complexities of any single program without discernible loss of efficiency, is a mischievous notion that has caused untold harm in our development. Our concern with the issue of the nature of social work competence requires that we reopen the whole question of specialization. Our justified disenchantment with a model of specialization based on fields of practice or specific methodology should not blind us to the possible validity of other alternatives. The problem-area approach to the analysis of social work practice developed under the leadership of Dr. Nathan Cohen represents an important contribution to this issue. In the problem-area formulation, the social work task with respect to a relevant social problem is first clearly specified, and within this specification strategies that draw upon the entire range of social work practice are designed to accomplish these tasks. It is a conceptualization designed to ensure that the contributions of social work shall be co-ordinated with and complementary to the work of other individuals, groups, and disciplines. The appeal of this approach is that it breaks down the social work mission into manageable units of attention and provides a framework within which we can begin to specify more precisely the range of competence required to execute our responsibilities.

If we should elect to move in this direction, the necessity to seek more effective ties between education and practice becomes imperative. The failure of the social work profession and social work education to provide the means whereby the graduates of its professional schools can continue to develop their professional competence constitutes a threat to the very existence of social work. That education is a time-limited stage which precedes one's entry into the real world of doing is a notion that fortunately is dying rapidly. A youthful and distinguished physicist at the California Institute of Technology commented recently that there were few, if any, specific facts that he had learned as a student which had any current validity. If this is not equally true of social work, it ought to be to a degree considerably greater than it is.

## *Meeting the Challenge*

The distinctions that once set the groves of academe apart from the marketplace are no longer real. General Motors and the National Institutes of Health have teaching faculties that are the envy of many a great university, and in turn the universities have become a vital and active force in the life of every major city. In the present day, competence in any field is not something to be achieved but rather a capacity that must constantly be renewed and re-established if it is to have any continuing relevance. We must accept the fact that learning and practice are inseparable—that we are all teachers and learners.

Neither is the realization of social work competence to be achieved only by going broader and deeper along familiar paths. A rhetoric or professional style conceived in our backwater days is hardly sufficient for the quickened pace of the marketplace. Understanding or relating to a hippie or any of the new breed of activists may not be quite the same thing as establishing a professional relationship with those docile clients encountered in the first year of social work training. Working with a board composed of clients is not quite the same thing as working with boards whose chairs were passed along with the family silver. Many of our traditional competences have continuing validity and an applicability we have only begun to realize. Other competences must be reworked and streamlined if they are to be applicable to the needs of our time. For example, a model of casework diagnosis and treatment that is predicated on five or six leisurely office interviews and a psychiatric consultation makes little sense in a crisis situation. Still other competences need to be invented and developed to extend our repertory. To achieve greater competence and relevance, we must succeed in orchestrating more effectively the many forces of the community that have entered the arena of social welfare.

The greater the complexity of any system, the greater the danger that the failure of any one part will throw the entire system into imbalance and ineffectiveness. This is as true of the helping systems of social welfare as it is of biological organisms. Unlike biological systems, most of our welfare helping systems lack any master gland that insures the necessary synchrony of the parts. They lack any inherent mechanism of adjustment by which that indispensable character of humanity and respect for the individuality as well as the sameness of man will be insured. Social work is eminently well suited for this task. Philosophically our roots are deeply embedded in those humanistic traditions that have steadfastly concerned themselves with the wholeness of man. This is not to suggest that we are alone in this commitment or that we are the only group that has acted in response to these convictions. Nevertheless, of all the professions, at our best we have demonstrated a fidelity of purpose and occupied a position that has bridged the abstract and the concrete. It is equally true that too often we have veered from this course, but the potential remains to be recovered.

There are many indications which suggest that social work is responding to this challenge. Elliot Studt [1] describes how social workers operating from the perspective of the California

---

[1] Elliot Studt, Sheldon C. Messinger, and Thomas P. Wilson, _C-Unit: Search for Community in Prison,_ New York: Russell Sage Foundation (1968).

prison system helped to change what was once a traditional prison whose function was primarily custodial into an effective rehabilitative experience. The activities of these social workers included components of casework, group work, and community organization. But it was an approach that was not the product of simple addition. It required the invention of new patterns of service delivery in which inmates and custodial staff as well as psychiatrists and dentists committed themselves to a rehabilitative strategy that transcended the ideologies of any one of them. It was for a time a most effective program. What Dr. Studt demonstrated, however, is that such a harmony of collective efforts is never fully won. It is an achievement that must be constantly worked at if the frictions, the deeply rooted habits and suspicions, and the never sufficient conditions for tasks given us are not to result in the loss of hope and creativity and ultimately the failure of our mission.

The capacity to work effectively in this context requires the development of a new order of social work competence, the acquisition of new knowledge, and the reinterpretation of our values. Social workers need not fear that in this search they stand in any danger of losing their identity. In those programs in which social workers have demonstrated these competences the stereotype of the determined do-gooder has faded. In the jargon of the marketplace we have become recognized as respected "fixers" and worthy allies. In an era of disillusionment and anomie we have attracted to our ranks an unprecedented number of creative and intelligent men and women drawn by the hope that this is where the significant action is and that ours is a mission worthy of their commitment. We must prove worthy of this commitment.

# Changing Concepts of Social Work Treatment and Prevention of Problems on a Community Level

## DUANE W. BECK

THE OBJECTIVE here is to achieve a higher degree of understanding of societal changes that indicate the need for changes in social services and in their delivery. The background and frame of reference are those of a social planning and community organization practitioner in a large, urban, metropolitan complex. The social conditions and problems discussed are those found in a large urban area and are typical of the metropolitan areas of the United States. These problems will be found also in slightly different ways in smaller urban areas.

There was a time when social work seemed to be the only profession directly concerned with the problems of the poor in our society, but over the past five years the interest of other professions has grown. Lawyers, clergymen, sociologists, political scientists, psychiatrists, psychologists, anthropologists, and many self-developed specialists are now very much concerned with and are making interesting contributions to the solution of many social problems. It is painful at times to hear their criticisms of social work, but we must be strong and secure enough to examine and then accept the negative comments of our allies.

Some of their criticisms are well founded, and they are instrumental in forcing the social work profession to re-examine what it is and how it goes about performing its tasks. It is true that for too long we have been concerned primarily with the development of remedial services that look after the individual or family only *after* the catastrophe or injury has occurred. None of the disciplines that come out of the field of social work can say this was not its primary concern at one time. Although we have had our social activists such as Jane Addams, we were primarily the profession that developed to ease the suffering of those who had some form of social disability.[1]

John Turner says that the social work profession has been concerned with the area of social problem management in that it has been occupied in developing techniques of dealing with individual dysfunction.[2] We talked for a good many years about prevention, but without some practical help from other professions and disciplines not much truly preventive of social problems could really be developed. It is only recently that our society has rethought the national policies of how we are to deal with the disabled of our society and society's disabling conditions that create individual dysfunction. The emphasis is now on the human being as a societal resource rather than as a social liability.

Two things have happened that have redirected our thinking.

[1] Nathan E. Cohen, "The Future of the Social Agency in a Changing Urban Society," a paper delivered at the National Conference on Social Welfare, Dallas, Texas, May 1967. Cohen describes social work as having two phases, the sociological and the psychoanalytical, the latter controlling the profession with a heavy emphasis on individual treatment.
[2] John B. Turner, "Relation of Health and Welfare Planning to Social Change and Social Development," *Social Work and Social Planning,* New York: National Association of Social Workers (1964), pp. 11–19.

One is that we can control and shape variables in a person's life, both those he inherits and those external forces in society that are at work upon him. Lindemann [3] and Caplan identify the interaction of internal and external factors and label it the "situational crisis." Erikson, who dealt with the same problem on a sociological basis, termed it the "identity crisis."

The second major factor is that we are now convinced we have the power within our society to change those things that produce stress and strain on individuals and create many social problems. Along with this idea came the recognition that in some instances it is not services that are needed but methods of influencing attitudes and ways of changing systems or institutions of our society. [4]

The concept of "systems dysfunction" brought to us by those interested in the field of community development has led to the development of a theory of how society and its institutions work to the disadvantage of some people in society. Community development is another form of community organization but has as its goals the solving of some of its basic problems that are central to any community. [5] Social work, having no monopoly on community organization, is accepting what other specialists in community organization are saying, and the joining of forces is taking place. Roland Warren says that commu-

[3] Erich Lindemann, "Mental Health and Environment," *The Urban Condition: People and Policy in the Metropolis,* Leonard J. Duhl, Ed., New York: Basic Books, Inc. (1963), pp. 3–10.

[4] Martin Rein and Robert Morris, "Goals, Strategies for Community Change," *Social Work Practice, 1962,* New York: Columbia University Press (1962), pp. 127–45. See also Thomas D. Sherrard and Richard C. Murray, "The Church and Neighborhood Community Organization," *Social Work,* Vol. 10, No. 3, July 1965, pp. 3–14; Martin Rein and Frank Riessman, "A Strategy for Antipoverty Community Action Programs," *Social Work,* Vol. XI, No. 2, April 1966, pp. 3–12.

[5] Turner, "Relation of Health and Welfare Planning. . . ."

nity development and social work share the same set of fundamental values and that community development and community organization are closely allied social work processes.[6]

The determination to change society and its systems has been developed into national policy and now manifests itself in many ways. Examples are found in the community action programs of the poverty program, the new experiment in comprehensive approach in the Model Cities Program,[7] and more recently the visible determination of the Public Health Service [8] to develop a coordinated planning approach to the solution of health problems in the community.

There has been so much written about the urban, metropolitan complexes and their social conditions and problems that it is not necessary to recount facts, figures, and reasons why our cities look as they do today. The recently published report of the United States Committee to the Thirteenth International Conference of Social Work, held in Washington, D. C., in September 1966, offers a concise summary of urbanization in the United States.[9] The document is a synthesis of much of the writing and work done by social scientists and social workers in this country, and not only gives the material in a concise, organized fashion but also furnishes a comprehensive bibliography.

[6] Roland C. Warren (ed.), *Community Development and Social Work Practice,* New York: National Association of Social Workers (1962).

[7] H. Ralph Taylor, et al., "Comments On the Demonstration Cities Program," *Journal of the American Institute of Planners,* Vol. XXXII, No. 6, Nov. 1966, pp. 366–76. See also *Improving the Quality of Urban Life: A Program Guide to Model Neighborhoods in Demonstration Cities,* USDHUD. Washington, D. C.: Supt. of Documents, United States Government Printing Office, 1966.

[8] James H. Cavanaugh, *Comprehensive Health Planning and Public Health Services Amendments of 1966* (PL 89, 749), USDHEW, Public Health Service (1967).

[9] Lawrence K. Northwood, *Urban Development in the United States: Implications for Social Welfare,* New York: United States Committee (1967).

*Mobility*

We are aware of the movement of people from rural areas because of the mechanization of agriculture. Many of these people are poor, have obsolete skills or no skills, and possess little education. They tend to move into areas where jobs exist because they are seeking to improve their situations but find that the technological advances of society have not provided a place for them. We are also aware of the movement of people from the central city to suburban areas as newcomers—the poor, both Negro and white—have moved into the older deteriorated and deteriorating areas of the city.[10] The burgeoning economy has permitted internal movement, much of which is being precipitated by the attitudes of the white majority and their biases toward nonwhites. Along with this we note the phenomenon of national industry, business, and government moving people from one part of the United States to another. Thus there are three distinct types of geographic mobility.

Geographic mobility is not the only form of mobility. The idealism of democracy still prevails in this country and along with it the individual is inspired to move up the social ladder. As conditions improve economically, people in skilled and semiskilled occupations have moved into areas side by side with people of the white-collar class who tend to have different attitudes and values about life and living. This social mobility has for many as great an impact as does geographic change.

The movement to cities of poorly equipped people and the

[10] Robert Gutman, "Population Mobility in the American Middle Class," *The Urban Condition: People and Policy in the Metropolis,* Leonard J. Duhl, ed., New York: Basic Books, Inc. (1963), pp. 172–83. See also Herbert Gans, "Effects of the Move from City to Suburb," *ibid.,* pp. 184–98.

movement of these people within the cities after they arrive has created an extremely fluid situation, one that most of the systems and subsystems that offer service programs in the community find difficult to deal with.[11] For example, in Atlanta there is an elementary school whose annual enrollment one year exceeded its capacity by 100 percent. This meant that during the school year as many people moved away from the community as were currently enrolled at the end of the year. If the system is trying to provide a service to these individuals, it faces an impossible situation because the individual has no continuity in the program.

It is not fair to blame a public school system for this mobility. In analyzing the matter we know that all types of governmental action—highway construction, urban renewal, ordinance enforcement—cause much of the internal movement.[12] A small portion of the mobility is caused by people fleeing one residence for another because of economic difficulties.

The major causes of mobility are produced by another system —urban renewal—which has as its goal the improvement of the physical environment and is usually concerned primarily with the central city and slums. Only after a sufficient period of time has elapsed can we be sure that this physical improvement will show itself to be mostly moving problem people from one area to another and speeding up deterioration in new areas of the community. It is now possible to think about concerted and comprehensive action.[13,14]

[11] Gans, *ibid.*

[12] Bernard J. Friedan, "Toward Equality of Urban Opportunity," *Journal of the American Institute of Planners,* Vol. XXXI, Nov. 1965, pp. 320–30.

[13] Robert C. Weaver, "Major Factors in Urban Planning," *The Urban Condition: People and Policy in the Metropolis,* Leonard J. Duhl, ed., New York: Basic Books, Inc. (1963), pp. 97–112.

[14] Nathan E. Cohen, "The Future of the Social Agency in a Changing Urban Society."

## *Intervention*

The word intervention is now used a great deal in the literature. I define this as purposeful activity designed to modify another's activity, whether it is that of an individual or institution. The concept implies that we as a nation have developed a national policy to prevent an increase in problem people in the country by merely making things available for them. Much of the research in the juvenile delinquency program and in other programs preceding the Economic Opportunity Act showed us that many people from all walks of life did not know what programs and services were available or that the services that we did have were not accessible to them because of problems of transportation, illness, lack of funds, or responsibilities in the home. Consequently, if we are going to intervene effectively we have to begin to reach out to the problem people and institutions and deal with them directly.

Various theories were developed about how we reach out. We see these ideas manifesting themselves most recently in what are called the Neighborhood Service Centers.[15] Experimented with first in the delinquency program and heavily funded by the poverty program, these are now becoming primary structures in some of the comprehensive mental health models that are being designed.[16] This structure is designed to provide information and referral services to assist people to use established agencies. In some instances, our reaching-out

[15] Robert Perlman and David Jones, *Neighborhood Service Centers,* Washington, D.C.: USDHEW, Welfare Administration Office of Juvenile Delinquency and Youth Development (1967).

[16] See Leonard J. Duhl, Jr., "The Changing Face of Mental Health" and "Planning and Poverty," *The Urban Condition: People and Policy in the Metropolis,* Leonard J. Duhl, Ed., New York: Basic Books, Inc. (1963), pp. 59–75, 295–304.

operation brought information and referral to the neighborhood resident in his home or on the street.[17]

Other methods have been discussed, and we hear of the Citizens' Advice Bureaus in England and the Ombudsman of the Scandinavian countries. In a recent publication Kahn explores the whole business of citizen information centers, going further by providing information for people in other income ranges.[18] Kahn and Gardner agree that the bigness of our society necessitates the use of complex systems by which we deliver our services and programs.[19] The complexity of institutions makes it difficult for the individual in our society to find what is there for his use.

The revelation that people, both poor and affluent, lack knowledge of community services has renewed the emphasis on how information and referral programs should be developed in a major metropolitan community. It has also placed a premium on skills in communication with the community.

That a large number of people do not know about services has brought other changes. The question has been raised about the adequacy of the existing institutions.[20] A number of theorists began to see that the systems that were in existence tended to protect themselves from overloads by not completely revealing themselves to the community. Along with this the Neighborhood Service Centers and other advocates began to point out

[17] Perlman and Jones, *Neighborhood Service Centers.*

[18] Alfred J. Kahn, et al., *Neighborhood Information Centers, A Study and Some Proposals,* New York: Columbia University School of Social Work (1966).

[19] *Ibid.;* and John W. Gardner, *Self Renewal: The Individual and the Innovative Society,* New York: Harper and Row (1963).

[20] Nathan E. Cohen, "The Future of the Social Agency. . . ." Cohen speaks of private agencies establishing boundaries to protect limited resources.

that a number of people had been illegally excluded [21] or were eligible but not participating because of the difficulty in becoming a part of a service system. As services are now being decentralized a new role has developed for the sponsor of decentralized multiservice centers. In the process of referring clients the new structures have encountered difficulty in getting other structures to accept clients.

*Advocacy*

This resistance to accepting problem people in established institutions developed a role within and outside the centers that has been called advocacy. Perlman and Jones state that many of the centers act as advocates to protect the client's interest and rights with respect to other agencies.[22] The second role that has developed is that these centers often seek to change another institution's procedures or policies so that clients will be better served and the change will set a precedent. The system of which the target institution is a part will thus modify all its policies based on these few precedents.[23]

This kind of thought process and experience has produced new types of institutions, some of which are professionally manned and some developed by citizens themselves, with or without the help of professional organizers. There are the Legal Assistance Services, which are dramatically different from the Legal Aid Societies in most cities. These Legal Aid Service

[21] Charles F. Grosser and Edward V. Sparer, "Legal Services for the Poor: Social Work and Social Justice," *Social Work,* Vol. XI, No. 1, January 1966, pp. 81–87.

[22] Perlman and Jones, *Neighborhood Service Centers.*

[23] Robert Morris and Robert H. Binstock, *Feasible Planning for Social Change,* New York: Columbia University Press (1966). See also Perlman and Jones, *Neighborhood Service Centers.*

Centers provide low-income individuals with legal service, while the low-income legal counselors are beginning to take action against other systems when they think that system has violated the legal or constitutional rights of the individual either in how he is brought into the system or how he is excluded after having been part of it.[24]

Other structures manned by low-income residents have been formed. Alinsky and Hagstrom have stated that the quality of "hopelessness" found among lower-income residents must be overcome as the society offers services and programs. They declare that the solving of the individual's problem goes hand in hand with the citizen's participation in the structure designed to modify systems and institutions. This is much the same concept that is dealt with in social casework. The client must participate in the treatment process or change does not take place. Alinsky and Hagstrom are saying that the individual shows strength and grows through his participation. These people have to be taught to participate and the professional has to let them then carry the action for themselves, whatever the action is that they devise.[25]

These structures have created conflict and hostility. The systems that provided services in the community were not accustomed to being overtly and hotly criticized by those who are, were, or are potentially clients. Professionals reacted defensively and tended to defend the method, function, or operation of their system. This defensive reaction made it easier for the organizers of social action groups to achieve their purpose and has been interpreted as a lack of care for people in the community.

[24] Grosser and Sparer, "Legal Services for the Poor. . . ."
[25] Author's Note: This is my interpretation of conversations with Warren Hagstrom and from reading various articles written about Saul Alinsky for popular consumption.

## Indigenous Workers

One of the results of the attempt to institutionalize the advocacy role led to the employment of aides in the poverty program, both for that purpose and to provide jobs for talented low-income people without training. Conflicts developed between employees of a system and the administrators. The roles of the new employees were not clearly defined. The employees themselves had self-conceived roles and many of them went to work organizing people for action in the low-income areas. It is not uncommon now to find that the system which employs individuals is being picketed by the groups organized by their employees.[26]

There is a different kind of conflict in many of the low-income areas, where the indigenous worker played a leadership role rather than an enabling role, a kind of activity contrary to professional social work training. Often the aides in the programs could get information more easily and organize groups much more quickly than could the trained professionals.[27]

Some of the criticism directed at the professional made it appear as though he had no role in the new programs. This criticism and position have been altered in the last year. The systems reacting to the criticism have moved to decentralize some of their programs. This decentralization has put workers

[26] George Brager and Harry Specht, "Mobilizing the Poor for Social Action," *Social Work Practice*, 1962, New York: Columbia University Press (1962), pp. 127–45. See also Perry Levinson and Jeffry Schiller, "Role Analysis of the Indigenous Nonprofessional," *Social Work*, Vol. XI, No. 3, July 1966, pp. 95–101; and Frances Fox Piven, "Participation of Residents in Neighborhood Community Action Programs," *Social Work*, Vol. XI, No. 1, January 1966, pp. 73–80.

[27] Harry Specht, "Community Development in Low Income Negro Areas," *Social Work*, Vol. XI, No. 4, October 1966, pp. 78–89.

more directly into contact with client populations where they live. It has made the worker more accessible to the client, and the worker has begun to gain a better understanding of the clients' life-styles by more intimately seeing their struggle for existence.[28]

## *The Growing Suburban Problem and Mental Health*

If we can project from these experiences with low-income groups to suburban middle-income areas, we can speculate on new techniques of service delivery and what kinds of service will be needed.

These services could be developed in a community mental health center—a type of multiple-service center. The fact of the matter, as we know well by experience, is that the middle- and upper-income groups have their life stress situations: a death in the family, a child starting school, a child getting into trouble, alcoholism of one of the adults in the family, a decision and the feelings around it in respect to an elderly member of the family, isolation from the community, and new surroundings because of forced relocation, just to name a few. It is quite possible that there would be a heavy emphasis on child-rearing problems and personal and family relationships. The problem of temporary care for children is just as acute with women in the work force in middle-income areas as it is in low-income areas.[29]

[28] Author's Note: The changing attitudes of workers and the increasing respect of clients for public welfare workers were pointed out at a recent seminar conducted for the author by both the workers and seminar participants who were employed in Neighborhood Service Centers. Northeast Child Welfare League Conference, April 1967, Hartford, Conn.

[29] Dwight W. Rieman, *Mental Health in the Community Health Program,* Austin: Hogg Foundation for Mental Health, University of Texas (1962).

The comprehensive community mental health program too has its difficulties in freeing itself from past traditions of the medical treatment model of mental health.[30] Most of the comprehensive mental health centers that are developing are still predicated on mental illness treatment with the primary occupation of providing beds, whether full time or part time, for sick people. The whole field of mental health is an area needing better collaboration between community social work and psychiatry.[31] Knowledge and understanding of community have not been thoroughly comprehended by those professionals with medical backgrounds coming into mental health.

The comprehensive community mental health center should have as one of its functions the precipitation of change in other institutions with which it is in contact. It could very well incorporate a new concept in locating and bringing cases into the community mental health center. It will be interesting to see whether or not mental health and psychiatry primarily can free themselves from their traditional backgrounds and become more than individual dysfunction management institutions.

Earlier, the new experimental program called Model Cities was mentioned. This program is still in its infancy with nothing but planning proposals sent to the Department of Housing and Urban Development. However, the philosophy that brought this program into being should be considered. Through this program the municipal governments are the prime contractors and are responsible for the planning and

---

[30] *The Community Mental Health Center,* Pamphlet USDHEW, USPHS, NIMH, Office of Public Information, Maryland, 20014.

[31] Leonard S. Cottrell, Jr., "Social Planning, the Competent Community and Mental Health," *Urban America and the Planning of Mental Health Services,* Vol. V, Symposium No. 10, New York: Group for the Advancement of Psychiatry (November 1964), pp. 391–402.

execution of the program. The funds for any piece of the program will be funnèled through a single central local body, thereby giving that source the power to make change by combining the planning and the funding leverage. The city will not be responsible for actually conducting any piece of the program. Adequate provision is made for contracting with other service bodies. However, the centralization of authority and the designation of city hall as a coordinating body puts a new twist on what role city governments will play in future social resource development within their communities.[32]

Looking further at Model Cities, one finds a heavy reliance on governmental services. It is an overt statement of policy that the public or tax-supported services rather than private agencies will play future major service provision roles. There are many who see this reliance on public services as a threat to the private agency, which it may well be if the private agency does not rethink its role in the provision of social services in the community.[33]

The role of experimentation and demonstrations that private agencies once felt was their strong point has also been preempted by the entry of federal resources into the social welfare arena.

The private social welfare agency has been accused of having moved away from the low-income group and providing more and more of its services for those who can pay part or all of the cost. It is true that agencies have had to make choices about

[32] See Model Neighborhoods' Program Guide, *Improving the Quality of Urban Life: A Program Guide to Model Neighborhoods in Demonstration Cities,* USDHUD. Washington, D. C.: Supt. of Documents, U. S. Govt. Printing Office, 1966.

[33] Nathan Cohen, "The Future of the Social Agency in a Changing Urban Society."

whom they will serve. It was (and is) an almost impossible task to develop individual treatment and mental health programs among the poor when it was an irrefutable fact that these programs could not deal with the other overwhelming and almost insurmountable problems that face the poor. Lack of income, adequate housing, education, jobs, and job skills could not be overcome by counseling.

It appears that we are ready for a merger of two philosophies, one that has been expressed in terms of service and one in terms of eliminating barriers to poverty (social change). The private agencies probably have as much skill as anyone in their work with the counseling service programs and with the community itself. The programs that are dealing with jobs and job training and income are necessary and coequal partners in any new push that would raise individual living levels. We are ready for a new kind of wedding of programs. Whether or not the community service centers with their multiple-service approach is the best way for this marriage to take place no one can yet say for certain.

There is one other factor that should be considered. The involvement of a general theory of systems and the trend to define problems first and then move to action has freed social planners from the shackles of traditional answers. The recent guaranteed income maintenance proposals are one result.

The national debate under way on a better form of income maintenance for low-income people started about three years ago when a leading conservative economist advanced an idea for a negative income tax to provide a basic income floor. The proposal was predicated on eliminating all kinds of subsidies—public welfare, social security, farm subsidies, public housing, and many other programs that had been built into our social welfare picture. The motivation of the individual who offered this first thought on negative income tax is questioned. However, the idea should be dealt with constructively and modified so that the system of providing basic income can be improved. Alvin L. Schorr, in one of the recent issues of *Social Work,* explores the number of ways in which society could offer a guaranteed income maintenance program.[34] He does not rely on the negative income tax as the only and best way of doing the job. He considers the rearing of children extremely important and includes children's payments as part of a guaranteed income maintenance program.

Whatever combination of programs is used to improve the income floor for everyone in this country, it is obvious that the trend is toward changing the present public welfare system.[35] Elizabeth Wickenden, among others, feels that services and money should not be separated.[36] In her estimation, the experiences over the last thirty years with the social security program indicate that more than money is required to eliminate poverty. Alan Wade recently stated that the fallacy of the "money-is-not-enough philosophy" is apparent because people cannot handle services of any kind until they have enough food

[34] Alvin L. Schorr, "Alternatives in Income Maintenance," *Social Work,* Vol. XI, No. 3, July 1966, pp. 22–29.

[35] "National Blueprint for Public Welfare," a reprint from *Indicators,* Nov., 1967. USDHEW, Supt. of Documents, United States Government Printing Office, Washington, D. C., 20402. See also *Having the Power, We Have the Duty,* a summary of recommendations to the Secretary of HEW by the Advisory Council on Public Welfare, Washington, D. C., June 1966.

[36] Elizabeth Wickenden is a consultant to the National Assembly on social legislation. She has made several presentations on the subject of income maintenance policies. Printed copies of her papers on the subject can be obtained by writing the Assembly, 345 East 46th St., New York, N. Y., 10017. (The author here is working from notes made during a CCAA, Inc., staff meeting of which Mrs. Wickenden was the discussion leader.)

to eat, enough clothing, and a proper, decent place to live.[37] Social workers may have to help decide the issue.

The discussion of the minimum income maintenance policy of the United States gives one every reason to believe that every other system will undergo similar introspection and examination. Systems examination is very much a part of regenerating the society in which we live. The systems have often reflected through their official rules, regulations, and even the legislation that sets them up, attitudes of the majority group in society. Individual citizens have found it difficult to deal with highly bureaucratized systems, whether public or private, and whether the individual is low, medium, or upper income.[38] Systems modification nearly always indicates that the leadership within that system must undergo an attitude and value change.

One of our quandaries in this whole question, however, is how to institutionalize the outside impact of third-party forces that will continue to modify the systems and their subparts. The social action device for organizing low-income citizens is certainly one method that has reached a minimal stage of institutionalization. Whether or not this type of organization for social action is to become a part of social work remains to be seen.[39] Members of the social work profession are generally employed by institutions which in the past, be they public or private, have too often represented a status quo situation in the community. The institutions have sought only minimal increases in money for services and minimal solutions to problems. The social work profession is by no means an indepen-

[37] Alan Wade, "The Guaranteed Minimum Income: Social Work's Challenge and Opportunity," *Social Work,* Vol. XII, No. 1, January 1967, pp. 94–101.

[38] Alfred Kahn, *Neighborhood Information Centers.*

[39] George A. Brager, "Institutional Change: Perimeters of the Possible," *Social Work,* Vol. XI, No. 1, January 1967, pp. 59–69.

dent group such as those of law and medicine. It is highly unlikely that the social work profession and the institutions it staffs will play a major role in the organization of social activist structures in the community. It is necessary for social action structures to make the critical impact according to the strategy and timing that they conceive for themselves. Organizations that are controlled by the conservative economic leadership of the community are not likely to continue to receive funds for operation if they are the ones that foment discontent, unrest, and criticism of the existing systems. It appears that the whole area of social action will be supported neither by government nor by the existing social welfare establishment,[40] but by those people who stand to gain the most from the change they are seeking to create in the community—the excluded members of society. Independent financing of this kind of activity is the only financing that will give a highly controversial structure freedom of action and strategy development.

We should keep in mind that social work *does* have a role, and like many other groups that are now involved in urban development has as its primary concern the individual in this society and the interdependence of individuals and their institutions. We are past the time when we as a profession are the only ones interested in social problems, and we must work with those other groups who are now entering the field, even those who are highly critical of us.

[40] Nathan E. Cohen, "The Future of the Social Agency. . . ."

# Deprivation Amid Abundance: Implication for Social Work Practice

## MYRTLE R. REUL

THERE IS a tendency to equate poverty and deprivation, as if the only deprivation were one of loss or lack of material wealth. The Conference on Economic Progress in 1962 used two terms to describe levels of income. Those families whose annual income before taxes was less than $4,000 were said to be living in poverty. They represented 23 percent of all American families. The conference classified the income between "poverty and comfort" as "the deprivation level of living." These were the families with annual incomes from $4,000 to $5,999. They represented nearly another 23 percent of the total population, which when added to those "living in poverty" gave nearly 46 percent of all families in the United States some stigma of financial deprivation.

### Kinds of Deprivation

Not only has there been a tendency to equate poverty and deprivation in one breath, but also to classify all those who are poor as being culturally or socially deprived and conversely all those whose income places them in the affluent category as being nondeprived. This is a myth that must be dissolved before social workers can meet their challenge.

A check of any standard dictionary shows that the word deprivation means (1) being deprived; (2) taken away from; (3) kept from having. It is in this light that I examine "Deprivation Amid Abundance," not merely financial deprivation. There are many kinds of deprivation—social, physical, economic, spiritual, cultural, emotional, and intellectual.

Man is a social being who needs to relate to his fellowman. If his opportunities for interaction are limited, if his socialization is impaired, then he is socially disadvantaged. If an individual is mentally or physically handicapped he is deprived, in that his physical or mental impairment keeps him from having the same experiences as the nonhandicapped. An individual may have known extreme emotional deprivation, which results in a lack of basic trust in others or in a poor self-concept. Financially such a person may be part of the affluent society, yet he is still deprived. There are many with great material wealth who have no personal philosophy, no purpose in life. They are bored. They feel life has no meaning for them. They are deprived spiritually. They may also be deprived emotionally.

The illegitimate child is deprived of his legal right to a name and to his legal heritage. There is always deprivation in the four Ds of the broken home: (1) death; (2) divorce; (3) desertion; and (4) disorganization. Anything that prevents a child from having a meaningful relationship with both parents is a form of deprivation, although physically the child may have adequate care.

Medically, the word deprivation is often used to describe an agent of disease. This is most clearly defined in the field of tissue nutrition. Prolonged deprivation of food brings about tissue malnutrition and eventually death by starvation. Deprivation of specific foods can be clinically diagnosed and labeled. Scurvy, resulting from lack of vitamin C, is a classic example.

## Maternal Deprivation

Next to economic deprivation, maternal deprivation is seen most often by social workers. Maternal deprivation was first discussed by Spitz in a study that aroused much debate.[1] Spitz said that when the mother is not present during a child's infancy and no adequate substitute takes her place there is a pattern of retarded development, listlessness, and dwindling energy that often ends in mental illness or even death. This is a phenomenon not of income or of class, but of the failure of the mother to give emotionally to her child or else to provide a substitute who can.

Certain kinds of psychological deprivation can also create irreversible physical stress. Deprivation, stress, and infections are not usually separate agents in the causes of disease. They are all part of one cycle—the breakthrough over the defenses of the body that overcomes its tolerances, beats down its resistance —in short, dangerously and perhaps fatally upsets the consistency of its internal environment. No matter which one of the three phases of the cycle—deprivation, stress, or infection— irritates a disease process or appears most plainly in it, the other two are always present.

## Effects of Physical and Emotional Deprivation Seen in Reading Retardation

Dr. Ralph B. Rabinovitch, psychiatrist and director at Hawthorne Center, Northville, Michigan, says that the most com-

[1] Rene A. Spitz, "Hospitalism," *Psychoanalytic Study of the Child,* Vol. I, New York: International Universities Press (1945), pp. 53–74.

mon single and immediate cause for referral to his clinic is academic or social difficulty experienced by children in school. He feels that this suggests the need for intensive study of the meaning of the school experience, ways in which it affects the child, as well as the influence of the child's capabilities and personality on the learning process. There are multiple areas of the child's functioning involved in academic learning. Disturbances in any of these may lead to symptoms of learning retardation or deprivation. Most important are (1) general intelligence; (2) specific capabilities; (3) developmental readiness; (4) emotional freedom to learn; (5) motivation; and (6) opportunity.

The deprived, affectionless child presents as his major symptoms (1) reduced capacity to establish depth relationships; (2) inadequate social awareness and identification; (3) inability to control impulses adequately; and (4) limited capacity for insight. In the thought process there is marked concreteness, with poor conceptualization, which limits fantasy life and creativity. Basic and rote learning are less affected. The problem of primary reading retardation is one of physical deprivation.[2] Such retardation apparently reflects a basically disturbed pattern of neurological organization. The cause is biological. Although definite statistics are not available, it is likely that the majority of children presenting total or severe reading retardation have a primary problem.

## Emotional Poverty Amid Abundance

Robert Leeper and Peter Madison, in their book *Toward Understanding Human Personalities,* give much food for

[2] Ralph B. Rabinovitch, "Reading and Learning Disabilities," *American Handbook of Psychiatry,* Vol. I, New York: Basic Books (1959), pp. 857–69.

thought when they point out that a vast majority of those in the affluent part of American society today are experiencing emotional poverty or deprivation.[3]   They say:

Ultimately this may be what lies back of many of our difficulties of modern life.   If so, it may explain, to a considerable degree, the selfishness and competitiveness that creeps into so many situations. People may be seeking big incomes, not because they enjoy great wealth as much as they are badly frustrated in their hunger for a meaningful life.   They know that a large income has been one means of securing such a measure of emotional vividness.

## Indirect Expressions of Emotional Poverty

The authors go on to give what they call some indirect expressions of the feeling of emotional poverty: (1) *Pseudohungers for food as an expression of emotional poverty.* "Craving for food that the individual does not really need and would not eat were it not for his emotional hunger." (2) *An increased demand for closer human relationships as one effect of emotional poverty.* "Dependency upon and the demand for more satisfaction from close human relationships than reasonably can be expected in a marriage or a friendship. Some people want others almost to revere them." (3) *Overdependence on sexual satisfaction as a compensation for emotional poverty.* (4) *The powerful and insistent demands of material comforts may be an expression of emotional deprivation in other respects.* "Many persons who study our society come to feel that our interest in material products of our technology far exceeds their value as a means to a fuller life." (5) *Much interest in violence (directly or through fantasy) may be an expression of emotional poverty.* "A survey of radio and tele-

[3] Robert Leeper and Peter Madison, *Toward Understanding Human Personalities,* New York: Appleton-Century-Crofts (1959), pp. 247–90.

vision programs reported that killings and attempted murders were the two most popular topics on seven stations which were watched for a period of one week. A total of five hundred and eighty-eight killings and/or other crimes were counted, that is eighty a day, or one every seventeen minutes day and night."

*Factors Productive of Emotional Poverty*

Leeper and Madison think there are certain factors productive of emotional poverty in our society:

(1) *Conformity pressures* in a country founded in part on a belief in rugged individualism. Each year it seems to become more difficult to be one's own individual self.

(2) *Blue-Ribbon Motivation:* The individual is asked to be on top in his field, regardless of what it is. Even hobbies often become competitive. One difficulty about blue-ribbon motivation is that it guarantees that most of the group will be losers.

(3) *Oversaturation of Major Interests:* There is an extensive concentration on one single activity.

(4) *The Neglect and Belittling of Concrete Perceptual Experiences:* Our culture has laid stress upon abstract knowledge and standardization. It has been forgotten that some of our emotional experiences spring from things around us that impinge directly upon us, that are perceived as having color, warmth, vitality and are likely to be as down to earth as the play of color in the fireplace, or the feel of wind and rain. There is even a lot of tacit disapproval of living in the present in our middle class culture. It is as if we had some leftovers from past religions which prohibit investing too heavily in present earthly pleasures.

The society in which we live influences everyone in it. To some extent it shapes young people in ways that add to their conflicts and their anxiety. The way a minority group is treated tends to produce economic deprivation, discouragement, and aggression. Children are aware of the inequality of fate that has placed them in a disadvantaged position. Such children may resort desperately to badness as the only compensation for their deprivation as well as the only language they know how to speak.

## Who Are the Disadvantaged?

There are presently three major kinds of poverty in the United States: (1) insular, which refers to a depressed area such as Appalachia, where work patterns have changed; (2) "case" poverty—chronic, long-term, intergenerational poverty; and (3) functional poverty—those individuals and families who do not live in the usual pockets of poverty or who are not chronically disabled but who may function emotionally, socially, and economically at the poverty level.

*Rural deprivation.* About 30 percent of the population of the United States lives in rural areas. This rural population is disadvantaged in numerous ways. Incomes of rural people, especially of farm people, are disproportionately low. Rural individuals by and large receive less formal education than do urban persons. Moreover, there are large numbers of functional illiterates in the rural population. Functional illiteracy means that the individual cannot follow written instructions.

Despite the fact of considerable nonagricultural employment among rural people, nonagricultural employment opportunities in rural areas pay less than those available in urban areas. Department of Agriculture economists have estimated that the volume of rural farm males unemployed in the United States exceeds one million.

Too often social workers have been concerned only with urban areas, and yet close to one-third of America's youths live in a great diversity of areas described as "rural." Only one-quarter of the people of the rural areas live on farms. The remainder live in small towns, villages, hamlets, residential sub-divisions, strip settlements, and isolated dwellings scattered over the countryside. Youths from such communities are less fitted for successful competition in our modern, urbanized society than their urban counterparts.

Research shows that both the educational attainment and educational aspirations of low-income farm youths differ from those of other youths. They assign less importance to educa-tion and fewer aspire to continue their education beyond high school. Dropout rates are comparatively high, reflecting the low educational level of parents. Since only a small minority of farm youths—perhaps only 10 percent—can expect to become operators of adequate-sized farms, the majority must seek other occupations. With the decreasing number of unskilled and semiskilled jobs, this means that all youths from low-income backgrounds are handicapped in competing for higher status occupations, and that farm youths are severely handicapped in occupational achievement if they do not foresee that they must prepare for nonagricultural employment.

*Deprivation among Spanish-Americans.* Poverty and de-privation are widespread among the Spanish speaking, both the 3,500,000 Mexican-Americans and the 750,000 Puerto Rican–American citizens. Even in similar urban areas, the Spanish speaking more frequently live in poorer housing, are more over-crowded, and have less adequate sanitary facilities than their neighbors. Educational levels among Spanish-American adults are between three to six years below those of the total white population. One-fourth to one-half of the Spanish-American adults are functionally illiterate and high school dropouts remain high among Spanish-American youths. With lower levels of education and lack of skill, the unemployment rates among Spanish-American males are three to four times higher than among other white workers.

*Deprivation among Negroes.* Much has been written on and said about the deprivation of Negroes in this country. Technological improvements in rural areas of the South have contributed to changes in the social structure of living for thousands of Negroes. Displacement of workers from agriculture and technological changes that have made farm tenants expendable have forced large numbers of Negroes into urban centers, both within the South and outside. The personal and social adjustment of these families have been greatly complicated because they bring with them their rural culture and they are less educated and trained for job competition. In many cases the adjustments to urban living are so difficult that families are more deprived than they were before their migration.

*Deprivation in the Southern Appalachian region.* Originally the Southern Appalachian area was settled mainly by families who wanted no part of life along the eastern seacoast. Some had been indentured servants, and they carried into the wilds of the mountains a deep hatred for their masters. Many had known religious persecution. They moved into the mountains asking only to be left alone with their beliefs in God. The majority of the early settlers in Appalachia had reasons to mistrust the outside world. Later they were further exploited when coal was discovered. Large urban corporations bought up or leased the land and brought in professional miners to "take work from" the original settlers, or so it seemed to them. Those early families felt exploited and ridiculed. They were resentful when those outside the mountains became more affluent financially. From this sort of experience they taught their children to be cautious, to reveal little of themselves, to mistrust the motives of those in positions of authority.

In Appalachia, as in certain other areas of the country such as Arkansas and South Dakota, there has been a limited amount of recent in-migration, although out-migration has been high. Low in-migration places the kinship family in a more powerful position than in areas where there is high in-migration. Another consequence of low in-migration is the standardization of taste, usage, and outlook. Old ideas are not exposed to the questioning of newcomers because there are no newcomers. The young people who stay in these areas find little that is objectionable in traditional standards—they can live with them. A third consequence is psychological. The dominant emotional tone tends to become pessimistic and backward-looking as trade centers decline and young people leave. The interest in community improvement lessens. People perceive that the force of change is out of their hands.

This example from the southern Highlander's culture would also apply to any deprived family. Mistrust of others derives from several sources. The most obvious is that their life experiences, which have been heavily weighted with rejection, have led them to expect further rejection. They therefore endeavor to avoid the repetition of the painful experience by rejecting a person before he has a chance to reject them. Their mistrust also derives from lack of confidence in their ability to carry usual social responsibilities. Because they have had little opportunity to acquire vocational, homemaking, or child-rearing skills, they develop a deep sense of inadequacy. They realize that these very inadequacies precipitate disapproval and criticism, and in an attempt to protect themselves they tend to avoid close contact with people outside the family. For the same reason, they are often reluctant to discuss their situation frankly with persons who endeavor to help them. Their fear of being criticized leads them to deny the existence of problems and to evade helping efforts.

*Deprivation among American Indians.* The combination of the American Indian's present deprivation and the historical exploitation of his race causes many of his current problems. The effects of poverty long experienced by the Indian are compounded by the indifference and apathy of the general public and by his own inability to articulate his needs through the press or the ballot box. Among the more than half-million Indians, over half are under 20 years of age.

Of all racial and ethnic groups in the United States, the most deprived are the American Indians. Their housing is the poorest. Many live in earthen hogans, floorless log cabins, or year-round in tents in the Dakotas. Many have never known the luxury of electricity. They carry their water from a river or stock-watering pond. Indians are the least educated of any group in America today and have the highest rate of unemployment. In Alaska it is 80 percent. Their health needs are also the greatest and their death rate is the highest.

Indians are caught between the culture of their people and the culture of the dominant society. Fifty years ago the federal government came into Indian communities and carried children off by force to be educated in distant boarding schools. The result was confusion, ambivalence, and immobilization for the individuals who are now the parents of today's schoolchildren. Many have a deep hatred for the dominant white society and contempt for themselves. It is difficult for such people to be trusting. It is difficult to believe under their circumstances that a social worker has any respect for their culture.

The Indian culture was a shame culture; a child was not

punished, but was shamed into obedience. He was taught by example. The Indian child today is surrounded on all sides with stigma that give shame and doubt to his own identification. From his grandfather he has heard stories of the time when Indians were great people, when they were free. In the history books of schools he attends he reads: "In that part of America which is now the United States the Indians had nowhere advanced beyond the stage of barbarism. They had no written language. Their only domesticated animal was the dog. Most of them knew how to raise corn, beans and squashes, and the more intelligent, like the Iroquois tribes of what is now New York State, had a crude sort of government. . . ."[4]

The preadolescent Indian child comprises the highest percentage of school dropouts of any race because he has two choices: (1) to identify with the dominant society and make a complete cleavage with his own heritage, or (2) to return to that heritage. Most young people unconsciously select the latter. Two of the chief problems facing these Indian youths are (1) acquiring an education and (2) developing a sense of cultural identity. They return to the reservation, to the hogan as did their grandfathers. There are many fatal accidents involving Indian youths. It is almost as if unconsciously they chose death as the solution to being trapped between the Indian culture of the past and the dominant culture of the present.

*Characteristics of deprivation.* MISTRUST OF OTHERS. Because deprived persons and/or their relatives usually have known discrimination, they tend to develop negative or hostile attitudes. Also, since they are often subjected to rejection by the community in which they live, they tend to isolate them

[4] David Muzzey, *A History of Our Country,* New York: Ginn and Company (1943), p. 35.

selves from their neighbors. The negative attitudes of the community toward these deprived families or individuals are likely to be heightened if the families belong to a race or a culture that differs from the predominant one. Although persons of minority groups are often subjected to rejection in society, the rejection is more overt if their standards of living or conduct deviate markedly from prevailing ones.

One of the chief characteristics of both adults and children who come from deprived backgrounds is their lack of trust in others. Erik Erikson in his book *Childhood and Society* points out that the first stage of personality development is trust versus basic mistrust.[5] The relationship with the parent, especially with the mother, grants permission to the young child to reach out and trust others. If the parent does not trust the outside world or strangers, the child, too, will lack trust. The individual who is always suspicious of the motivation of others is a deprived person, although historically there may have been a valid basis for his parents' mistrust.

FEAR OF AUTHORITY. Because of their extreme mistrust, deprived persons have an exaggerated fear of authority. All persons have some fear of authoritative agencies, particularly of the courts. Members of deprived families, however, have greater fear. They feel threatened by persons who have limited legal authority and whose approach is nonauthoritative. They are often afraid of their social worker regardless of the agency represented. They have a distorted view of their relationship to community institutions and endow them with greater powers than they actually have.

Members of socially deprived families often have strong feelings of anger, aggression, and hostility intermingled with their

---

[5] Erik Erikson, *Childhood and Society,* New York: W. W. Norton and Company (1950), pp. 219-33.

mistrust and fear.   These hostile feelings, which are natural reactions to their deprived social status, vary considerably, both in intensity and form of expression.   Some persons are openly hostile and aggressive, while others attempt to hide their negative feelings behind a facade of friendliness and extreme politeness.   Another way to mask true feelings is with humor, to play the clown, the comedian who amuses his audience at the same time he is insulting them or others.   Some comedians are very caustic or sadistic in the name of humor.   A joke, story, or pun becomes the avenue to release personal hostility and anger. The anger stems not only from current dissatisfaction, but also from the painful and unhappy experiences suffered throughout life.   Often these resentments go back to early childhood when such individuals were exposed to neglect, abuse, or abandonment by their own parents, or they can go back earlier to the treatment their parents received.

HOPELESSNESS.   Deprived persons have a sense of hopelessness that underlies all other feelings.   Many of the parents of today's deprived children suffer from a deep feeling of depression and their acting-out behavior is an attempt to ward off such depression.   They find temporary escape by going on a drinking or spending spree, by sexual promiscuity, by fighting, or by engaging in delinquent acts.   Their acting-out behavior may also be a case of displacement or projected hostility that cannot be expressed toward the actual source.

PROJECTED ANGER.   Traveling as migrant farm laborers with the different agricultural streams in the United States, my husband and I saw anger projected onto persons whose situation had nothing to do with the actual cause of frustration.[6]   An example of this was a Mexican-American father we met in a

[6] Myrtle R. Reul, *Where Hannibal Led Us,* New York: Vantage Press (1967).

western state. He had promised his wife and children that when they were paid at the end of the week he would take them to a certain little restaurant. They had seen it from the street, with tables prettily decorated and patrons seemingly having a good time. On Saturday the family "dressed up." When they arrived at the door they were turned away, although they could see empty tables. The owners said they were "too large a party" to be served that day. To the family it seemed he said, "The likes of you are not allowed here."

How does a man under these circumstances save face in the eyes of his wife and children? Especially how does he save face in a culture in which he is the undisputed head of his household? How does he answer their question of "Why?" How does he hide his disappointment? He could not express his anger to the owner or he might have been jailed. He masked his hurt as they walked away. His anger was there, a sullen deep anger that multiplied each time he recalled the experience. He was reinsulted. He remembered standing in the doorway surrounded by his children, asking permission to be seated and to order food. His anger had to be expressed. He bought two bottles of cheap wine and returned to the grower's housing. Under the influence of alcohol his anger was released. He became violent. He kicked out screens, broke furniture and windows. He was not angry with the grower. In fact, he rather liked his employer, but his employer was part of the affluent society and could go to any restaurant and not be turned away. So the man vented his rage. If we can identify with this father for a few minutes, perhaps we can sense some of the helpless frustration he felt. How do you think you would feel if you were in his place? What would you do? Do not be too certain that you are not capable of such violence!

As helping people, social workers may be on the receiving

end of projected hostility. Sometimes we are the first individuals in the life of this person interested enough to express concern, to listen to the frustration.

SUPERSTITION. The child of the poor is quite likely to have been born into a family in which the parents too were born into a similar background. The impact of the experience begins even prior to birth. The hope of improvement is slight in those who are seriously deprived. Their hope must be stimulated before they can be drawn into active work on their own problems. They may not see that they are in any position to help themselves, but it can also take some other form. The concept of superstition in folk culture is one that social workers should understand.[7] The concept of the evil eye is an unconscious fear of succeeding. The individual has a strong need to fail. He believes if he succeeds too much he will set himself apart and others will be envious of him. If his associates are envious of him, they will wish him ill. He believes they have the power not only to make the wish, but also that their wish is a "magical wish" and he will experience misfortune. Under these circumstances it is far better for him to be poor because he knows those who are very poor envy those who have. Those who do not succeed envy those who do. It is believed by his culture that it is safer to be envious than it is to be envied. Not only is it dangerous to be in a position of being envied, it is lonely. One is set apart from one's family, neighbors, friends, or associates. It is felt that one must be vain and endowed with self-importance, a virtual "strutting peacock" to even want to be different. This means that such an individual must think himself superior. In the mountains it is often said, "He thinks he is

[7] Myrtle R. Reul, *Level of Expectation Among Minority Groups.* Mimeographed Colloquium presented for the Michigan State University School of Social Work, April 13, 1965, pp. 13–15.

too good for the rest of us. It was good enough for his pappy and it should be good enough for him."

Sometimes this concept of meekness and acceptance of one's place in life becomes involved with religious convictions. "The poor will inherit the earth, blessed are the poor." The Biblical quotation is translated from "the poor in spirit" to the financially poor. If the social worker is not aware of these basic concepts, which are part of the frame of reference of the client, the worker may describe an attitude as apathetic when it is anything but apathetic.

One often-made generalization is that deprived people are apathetic. There is apathy among the deprived, but not all that appears to be apathy should be defined as such. It could be that the individual is conserving his physical and psychic energy for things that he considers to be much more important than those that are being assessed as important by others outside his culture.

KINSHIP FAMILY TIES. While it is the pattern in deprived families to form a closely knit circle, chiefly for the purpose of protecting each other from outside interference, it is also the folk culture among the Spanish-Americans, Appalachian Highlanders, Indians, and Negroes to have strong family ties. It is important for social workers to know whether these self-contained families are an indication of deprivation or whether they are the strength of the culture. Another general sweeping comment made about deprived families is that they have few friends and little contact with social groups.

The Spanish-American culture, either from the Mexican heritage or the Puerto Rican heritage, is an example of the kinship family. In the Spanish culture the strongest feelings of belonging are found within the family, not the nuclear family, but the kinship or extended family. When the Spanish-American speaks of his family he means his parents, in-laws, uncles, aunts, cousins, children, and godparents. Godparents— *"compadres"*—are selected by parents for their children at the time of birth, baptism, or first communion. Obligations of godparents include providing assistance to the child's parents as well as giving direction and affection to the child. This gives an extension of the family in the form of more than one set of parents. The biological parents consult their children's god-parents about all important decisions and they, too, view the godparents as part of their family.

In the Spanish culture the older members of the family hold a revered position. They gain wisdom with age. For a Spanish-American to institutionalize such a relative, even to hospitalize him, is very difficult because it is not part of his culture. There is a strong need to keep the family together, physically as well as emotionally. At an early age a child learns respect for his elders. Above all else, he is taught to honor and defend his family. He is also taught to defend himself in a hostile world so that he can maintain his dignity as an adult. Every Spanish-American child must learn a complex set of rules as they apply to his own culture and as he will be viewed by those outside his culture.

Spanish-Americans also know discrimination, and as with the Negro child and the Indian child, the Spanish-American child at an early age learns how to cope in the dominant society. He learns how to react toward authority. He learns how to mask his true feelings. He learns whom he can trust among his own kind and what he can say and do in his own home. With this sort of early childhood conditioning it is not surprising to find that individuals who have learned to have a limited amount of trust in others, regardless of their race, are mistrustful of neigh-bors, employers, physicians, nurses, social workers, school teachers, public officials, and others. In their dealings with health and welfare agencies these families may express interest in the services offered, but they tend to avoid personal involvement, and often fail to follow through on plans that have been carefully worked out with them.

## *Implications for Treatment*

Because of inadequate parental care and guidance in early years, the person who is deprived emotionally retains many infantile attitudes and ways of behaving. His responses are often more appropriate to the preschool age of development than to the adult level. He has difficulty in deferring gratification, in making judgments about money and other practical matters. He is selfish, self-centered, and tends to get into trouble. Clinically one would say this person has poor ego development and therefore is at the mercy of his impulses. The nature of his problem implies the need for experiences and guidance that will foster new ego development.

Basil Bernstein in his "Social Class, Speech Systems and Psychotherapy," delivered originally as a paper to the British Association for the Advancement of Science on his research with the lower working class in England, reminds us that a deprived client's communication may seem to be inadequate.[8] He will have a low level of insight. He may seem to be negative and passive, thereby forcing the therapist or caseworker into taking a more dominant role. Above all, the therapist will meet an unwillingness on the part of the client to transform his personal feelings into unique verbal meaning. Such a client will have difficulty in verbalizing his personal

[8] Basil Bernstein, "Social Class, Speech Systems and Psychotherapy," in Frank Riessman, et al., eds., *Mental Health of the Poor,* New York: Free Press of Glencoe (1964), pp. 194–204.

experience and in understanding or accepting communications which refer to the source of his motivation. Bernstein points out graphically that language has never been perceived by such an individual as an important media for describing feelings. "Thus a special group of defense mechanisms are seen. These defenses include denial, disassociation and displacement rather than the more elaborate defenses which rely upon verbal procedures, such as rationalization." The defenses as presented by the client will help to shape the type of psychotherapy or casework which is offered.

## *Implication for Social Work Methods*

Social work treatment, which seemingly has been the most successful in working with deprived individuals, regardless of race or circumstances, has featured those programs that include (1) reaching-out procedures; (2) group procedures; and (3) co-operative endeavors.

*Reaching-out procedures.* The social worker reaches out to the client geographically as well as emotionally. In the early contact the worker attempts to gain an understanding of the family's deprivation. At this stage it is necessary to demonstrate interest and concern rather than to express them verbally. Such demonstrations can be shown through arranging for medical care or by straightening out misunderstandings with school, employer, or with a public welfare agency. Often it is desirable to accompany the client to an agency or an institution. This helps to demonstrate real concern and to help reduce the client's fear of authority. During the early period of contact, deprived clients continue to expect disapproval, criticism, and rejection. They may engage in many maneuvers, such as breaking appointments or expressing a wish to end the contact in order to test the social worker's interest. In this relationship, as in others, they tend to reject quickly in order not to be rejected. They need considerable time in which to overcome their mistrust and to accept the social worker's support and help. Some will never learn to trust.

The worker's aim in treatment is to help such clients learn to handle their affairs and their personal relationships with greater responsibility. As indicated earlier, many were deprived of guidance and training in their early years and, as a result, are arrested in their emotional development. Some are able to reach a higher level of maturity through a helping relationship that provides both acceptance and stimulus for further growth.

*Group procedures.* Group procedures have been found to be especially effective with persons from deprived backgrounds. Individuals with similar problems and attitudes are brought together for educational, recreational, or counseling experiences and they gain confidence from each other. Supported by fellow members of their group, they feel freer to express negative feelings and to expose their own weaknesses. They are often able to complain about things they would never be able to talk about with a caseworker in the one-to-one relationship.

Through the exchange of ideas, opinions, and experiences, group members lose some of their sense of being different from everyone else. The discussions often serve to correct some of their distorted views. There is, however, a tendency to intellectualize and there may not be as much personal insight as would be hoped by the professional staff member.

*Co-operative Endeavors.* The number and severity of problems faced by deprived individuals require a battery of com-

munity services and resources.   While in the past five years
there has been an increasing trend for agencies to join efforts to
reach deprived families, each community must be even more
imaginative with new and different combinations of agency services.   Volunteer workers as well as staff members in health
and welfare agencies can make a more significant contribution
in their rehabilitative efforts if the usual traditional lines of
agency can be broken and if more of the comprehensive mental
health plan can be introduced.   Community services and
resources needed by nearly every deprived family include such
diversified areas as (1) individual counseling; (2) health services; (3) financial assistance; (4) housing; (5) recreational
opportunities; (6) vocational guidance; (7) training in homemaking and skills in parental education; (8) legal consultation;
and (9) spiritual guidance.

Within this pattern of need there is a place for churches,
schools, libraries, employers, union and civic groups, private
agencies, and public agencies to play an important role in
providing positive experiences and in reducing negative attitudes.

## The Role of Community Planning

Regardless of the agency that spearheads the effort, community planning should be broad and deep, with all segments of
the citizenry represented.   A successful citizens' advisory group
for any planning must represent citizen interest.   The major
role of such an advisory committee is to gather facts in order to
forge a common community goal.   After a committee has found
the facts, all related public and private agencies must be included to carry through the program.   Since broad programs
often involve legal and financial problems, such key people as

state legislators and local councilmen should be included. Goals need to be set and priorities determined. Agencies may need to change the emphases of their programs, assume new roles, transfer functions, and otherwise alter their activities to achieve a common goal.

One community where I attempted preventive work in the area of juvenile delinquency has a co-operative project among the probate court, the public schools, and the mental health clinic in which group and individual counseling are being conducted with potential school dropouts.

In another community, staff members of the family service agency, the public school, the police department, the mental health clinic, and the Council of Churches, representing social work, education, nursing, religion, psychology, psychiatry, and police administration, are planning to do group counseling as part-time staff in a Big Brother agency.

Efforts in the past have been aimed largely at changing individual personality. Recent theory has indicated that changing the social situation may be more strategic. Intervention must occur simultaneously at many points. Agencies with different goals and representing different skills and disciplines must re-examine their goals. If planning is to be effective, change and adaptation will have to take place—in welfare and employment services, in educational institutions, and in political structures. Undergirthing every comprehensive project must be constant evaluation.

There has been a tendency in the past for communities to view most situations of deprivation as temporary. There is still, for example, a tendency to view the needs of the migrant worker and his family in this way. Year after year the same needs are seen in communities that viewed them last year as temporary, so no long-range plans were made beyond the immediacy of the present problem. Communities can no longer afford this sort of attitude. Deprived individuals, whether financially or emotionally deprived, will be with us always. Every community must look at the problem in its entirety and within its proper scope. This is where a broad interdisciplinary approach is needed that calls for new patterns of community planning. Some problems can be handled at the local level, others need state or federal intervention. This is not so much state or federal financing, as state and federal planning that creates more uniformity. Again referring to the needs of migrants, the number-one problem is education for the children. Much of that problem could be solved if there were uniformity of educational standards between states or even within a single state.

Along with community planning, there needs to be a more sensitive awareness of the cultural values of America's various racial and ethnic groups and the contributions of their differences. Social workers, counselors, educators, physicians, psychiatrists, psychologists, lawyers, religious leaders, personnel officials, and all other helping persons will continue to be faced with the dilemma of conflict and tension created between the personality structure of their clients and the expectations of the dominant middle-class values. The adaption that members of an ethnic group make will be dependent, to a large extent, on the manner in which they resolve their cultural conflicts and meet their new situation. This means that the community, as well as the individual social worker, will need to have more respect for individual differences.

*General References*

Burchinal, Lee G., ed. *Rural Youth in Crisis, Facts, Myths, and Social Change.* Washington, D. C., U. S. Department of Health, Education, and Welfare, 1965.

Caplovitz, David. *The Poor Pay More.* New York, The Free Press of Glencoe, 1963.

Caudill, Harry M. *Night Comes to the Cumberlands.* Boston, Little, Brown, and Company, 1963.

Conference on Economic Progress. *Poverty and Deprivation in the United States: The Plight of Two-Fifths of a Nation.* 1001 Connecticut Avenue, N. W., Washington 6, D. C., April, 1962.

Davis, Allison, and John Dollard. *Children of Bondage.* Washington, D. C., American Youth Commission, 1940.

Erikson, Erik. *Childhood and Society.* New York, W. W. Norton and Company, 1950.

Gittler, Joseph B., ed. *Understanding Minority Groups.* New York, John Wiley and Sons (Science Editions), 1964.

Gordon, Margaret S. *Poverty in America.* San Francisco, Chandler Publishing Co., 1965.

Handlin, Oscar. *Newcomers: Negroes and Puerto Ricans in a Changing Metropolis.* Cambridge, Mass., Harvard University Press, 1959.

Kluckhohn, Clyde, and H. A. Murray, eds. *Personality in Nature, Society and Culture.* New York, Knopf, 1953.

Leeper, Robert, and Peter Madison. *Toward Understanding Human Personalities.* New York, Appleton-Century-Crofts, Inc., 1959.

Lewis, Oscar. *The Children of Sanchez.* New York, Random House, Inc., 1961.

Lewis, Oscar, *Five Families.* New York, Basic Books, 1959.

MacIver, R. M., ed. *The Assault on Poverty and Individual Responsibility.* New York, Harper and Row, 1965.

Meissner, Hanna H., ed. *Poverty in the Affluent Society.* New York, Harper and Row, 1966.

Padilla, Elena. *Up From Puerto Rico.* New York, Columbia University Press, 1958.

80 *Deprivation Amid Abundance*

Proctor, Samuel D. *The Young Negro in America: 1960–1980.* New York, Association Press, 1966.

Rabinovitch, Ralph. "Reading and Learning Disabilities," *American Handbook of Psychiatry*, Vol. 1, New York, Basic Books, 1959, pp. 857–69.

Reul, Myrtle R. *Where Hannibal Led Us.* New York, Vantage Press, Inc., 1967.

Riessman, Frank. *The Culturally Deprived Child.* New York, Harper and Brothers, 1962.

Riessman, Frank, Jerome Cohen and Arthur Pearl, eds. *Mental Health of the Poor.* New York, The Free Press of Glencoe, 1964.

Ross, Arthur M., and Herbert Hill, eds. *Employment, Race and Poverty.* New York, Harcourt, Brace, and World, Inc., 1967.

Spitz, Rene A. "Hospitalism," in *Psychoanalytic Study of the Child*, Vol. 1, New York, International Universities Press, 1945, pp. 53–74.

Wakefield, Dan. *Island in the City.* Boston, Houghton Mifflin, 1959.

Weller, Jack E. *Yesterday's People.* Lexington, University of Kentucky Press, 1965.

Will, Robert E., and Harold G. Vatter, eds. *Poverty in Affluence.* New York, Harcourt, Brace, and World, Inc., 1965.

# Changing Concepts of Social Work Treatment of the Multiproblem Client

## NORMAN A. POLANSKY

ALTHOUGH OUR TOPIC is the "multiproblem client," it is clear that we use this label only as a convenient way to grasp the issues to be discussed. As we all know, the term hardly refers to a single disease entity. Worse, it deliberately begs the question: to whom is the client a problem? Related, of course, is the question of why he has, or is, so many problems, a question of great significance for treatment.

We are left, then, with an indistinct vision of a congeries of maladaptive behaviors—physical and emotional manifestations of which some are hardly able to be dignified as symptoms, sins of commission, and lacks of virtues of omission—and a general incitement to resign from the profession of social work. Since the impression is so vague, it might help to begin with a concrete case description. The aims of this are threefold: to give us a common frame of reference for our theoretical discussions, to revive in our minds some of the aura about such cases that is all too easily repressed when one leaves them behind,

Prepared for the NASW Southern Regional Institute, Birmingham, Alabama, June 18–23, 1967. Preparation of this paper was supported by a grant from the United States Children's Bureau to the School of Social Work, The University of Georgia.

and to illustrate some of the more general points to be made later.

## A Rural Multiproblem Family

Most of what is known about the multiproblem family, as with most of what is known about casework, comes from work in urban agencies. This is because in the cities there has been the greatest concentration of trained personnel and the greatest opportunity for interstimulation. Yet the type of case under consideration is by no means confined to the city. The following case turned up in our current work on child welfare problems in rural Appalachia. The dictation is from visits (can they really be called interviews?) conducted by my colleague, Christine DeSaix.

The County Department of Public Welfare director and Mrs. Parson, a caseworker, had talked with Mrs. Moore about the study and had scheduled an appointment for today. The DPW record contains extensive background information on Mrs. Moore in the record of Mary Brown, her mother. Twenty-five-year-old Mrs. Moore is the mother of three children born out of wedlock and two children born after her marriage to Don Moore.

Hattie Moore's children came to the attention of the agency in 1963 when she left two toddlers and a tiny baby with the Browns. Hattie could not be located, and the children were suffering from such low standards of care that the DPW initiated proceedings to have them declared abandoned and placed in adoption. When Hattie learned of this action, she returned to the Fowler community. At the time she was pregnant by Mr. Moore, subsequently marrying him and moving in with the Browns. Reports on the condition of the children indicated that they were receiving practically no care from Mrs. Brown, who had no diapers for any of the children, and none of them was toilet trained. There was no heat in the house and the children were running around naked from the waist down except for the baby, who was in a bed covered with an old rug.  Following this threatened action, Hattie's younger sister, who is three years younger than she and married, took the baby and has kept him ever since.

Hattie's sixteen-year-old sister, Ella Brown, is in the state training school because of truancy.  She was "walking the roads" and authorities feared that she might get into "trouble."  The judge ordered her to the state training school.  Mr. Brown defied the order, took her, and left the community.  They were later apprehended and Ella was admitted to the state training school.  Mr. Brown then disappeared and has not been heard from since.  Mrs. Brown applied for AFDC for herself and the two younger children: Alice, twelve, and Joe, eleven.

In the Brown-Moore home at the present time are eleven people: Mrs. Brown; her two minor children; her twenty-two-year-old son, Cloy, and his retarded sixteen-year-old wife; Mr. and Mrs. Moore; Mrs. Moore's two children born out of wedlock; and two children by Mr. Moore.  The only reliable income is Mrs. Brown's AFDC grant. Mr. Moore works sometimes "in lumber" and Cloy Brown is unemployed.

It was necessary to park the car and walk about one-half mile up a muddy, one-lane road to the house.  An old-model car was sitting in the yard.  Mrs. Parsons explained that Mr. Moore had received $100 in severance pay from the furniture plant and had promptly bought the car.  They didn't have money for insurance so they couldn't drive it.  The ground around the house was rock-hard despite the rain.  The house stood several feet above the ground and there was debris and trash under it.  I counted six dogs.  While I warded off the vicious dogs with my purse, Mrs. Parsons went to the door.  The small porch was reached by a dilapidated stairway with every other step missing.  Hattie opened the door with 4½-year-old Caleb darting from behind her.  He was barefooted and it was cold outside so Hattie called for him to stay in.  Only one room of the four-room, unpainted house was heated.  This room contained three beds, a broken-down sofa, an overstuffed chair, a little wooden chair with the legs cut off, and a contraption covered with cardboard, serving both as a table and woodbox.  The room was heated by a pot-bellied stove on which a pan of water boiled. Hattie's mouth was filled with snuff and it was running down the

corners of her mouth.   She spent much time during the brief interview moving back the lid to the stove and spitting into the fire,
producing a loud sizzle.

The most pathetic sight in the room was a tiny ten-month-old
baby sleeping on a cot.   She had her little bottom in the air, expos-
ing a soiled, black diaper.   Hattie said that she was the smartest
child she had.   The baby could stand and almost walk, and had
climbed onto the cot when tired.   The 2½-year-old girl was sitting
on the sawed-off chair near the stove.   She was fully dressed in a
very thin summer dress but she did have shoes, socks, and a sweater.
She had nice features and would have been a beautiful child except for a bad cold, a very dirty face, and hair that was so matted
and dirty that it stood straight up.   She kept a bottle in her mouth
throughout the interview.

The disorder and dirt in the house were unbelievable.   There was
clothing lying all over, even mixed in with the wood.   When Hattie
put wood on the fire, a shirt was between the pieces and I am sure
if we had not retrieved it, the shirt would have been burned.

Mrs. Parsons introduced me.   She said that I was from the Children's Bureau and that I was going to see a number of people in
Fowler to see how they, especially the children, lived.   Mrs. Parsons
said that she knew Hattie had had a pretty rough time, and that they
had thought perhaps she would like to have someone she could talk
to.   Hattie answered that she sure had had it rough, and that she
didn't know what she was going to do.   Hattie said that she had
gotten a cold and had such a sore throat that she could hardly talk.
Several times during the interview she opened her purse and took
out a bottle of "cough medicine" and took a swallow.   The little girl
tried to get in her purse to get some and Hattie said that she was
"crazy about it and would drink a whole bottle."   We talked about
the adjustment of the children, and if Dorothy liked school; without answering, Hattie again complained of her throat.   Mrs. Parsons asked if Dorothy was glad to get back to school in Fowler.
Again, Hattie complained of her throat.   It seemed that each time
we asked questions about the children, she could not answer.   She
said that she was looking for work and expected to get a job at the
shirt factory once she got over her cold.   Mr. Moore had found
work in "pulp" right away.   Just as soon as he gets paid they ex-

pect to get insurance for their car so they can drive it and then Hattie can go to work.

Two weeks later, Hattie had very little reaction to my presence. When I first walked in, she said she had been expecting me. I answered that I was glad that they were home, although I had not heard from her. I took a chance on finding them home. Hattie explained that the card that I sent had been lost. Mrs. Brown added that everything gets lost in the house and that she couldn't stand it anymore. She explained that eight people slept in one room, her son and daughter-in-law in one bed, Alice, her twelve-year-old daughter, in a single bed, and she in the big bed with her son and two of Hattie's children. She measured on her hand how far the springs came out of her mattress and showed me a scratch on her leg where she had been hurt by them. The family cannot allow the stove to burn all night because of fire hazard. Hattie told me that one day the roof caught on fire three times. She showed me a large place in the ceiling where the cardboard-like roofing had been torn off to stop one of these fires. There was nothing between the room and the outside roofing.

Mrs. Brown is a dark, thin woman who looks much older than her forty-eight years. She kept her place behind the stove and almost constantly mumbled about not being able to live with all these people in the house. She didn't know what she was going to do since they had all moved in on her again. She seemed sad and bitter that Mr. Brown had left her with the two children. Now everything was on her.

When Peggy got up, she had a white, sticky substance all over her face and on her arms up to her elbows. Her hair still stood on end. Hattie explained that she had been eating powdered milk from the box. Hattie tried to pick it off but it was dried and scaly, and hurt the little girl. It was necessary to warm water on the stove. There was a search for soap, and one of the children came up with a new bar of Dial they had found in a bag on Mrs. Brown's bed. Mrs. Brown jumped from her place by the stove and ran to rescue "her bar of soap." They finally found a little piece of soap and washed the powdered milk off. The child was scrubbed so hard that her skin was almost raw.

Hattie had removed the iron skillet from the stove and set it on the "table." When she started to wash Peggy she moved the iron skillet and sat the little girl in the spot where it had been. Although the child had no pants on and the spot was hot, Hattie scolded her for complaining about her bottom. Hattie never finished washing her. Before she was through washing she left her and found a brush and combed only one side of her hair. This side lay down reasonably well while the other stood straight up. She was sitting perilously on the edge of the woodbox table. The water that was being used to wash her had been used to wash the other child. It was too hot, almost boiling, when Hattie put it in the middle of the kitchen floor. When I quietly warned Hattie, she kicked the pot back under the stove for someone else to wash in later. There was much to-do about cleaning the children, and all the time Hattie was running to the window to look for her husband. While she was washing the children she washed her own face but did not change her clothes, which were covered with snuff drippings. She explained to me that her husband was "mean about the children being clean." She had to have them washed each day when he comes home. And so forth. . . .

Among the three generations of this unfortunate family there is enough work for a whole bureaucracy of experts—delinquency, infant malnutrition, emotional disorder, mental subnormality, inadequate income, and more. It is hardly surprising in the midst of all this that the husband who was so "mean about the children being clean" soon deserted. The circumstances were rather interesting, since he did love his children, although he told a friend that sometimes he felt as though he would have to kill "the whole pack of them." His friend advised him to leave, since he was obviously nearing the end of his rope. It would be interesting to know how many of the "absent fathers" about whom we so often hear depart not because they have *no* standards, but because they still have some.

This example is useful because it pointedly raises a question: what sort of personality would you expect in a child whose grandmother behaved like Mrs. Brown and whose mother behaved like her daughter, Hattie?

With all the talk of guaranteed annual income, it has become popular in some quarters to think of the multiproblem client as a victim of fate. Although I would not argue against the need for better income-maintenance programs or that our public welfare system is abominably underfinanced, I believe that professional social workers cannot overlook the job that will still remain—if only because they know that it exists also in many middle-income families, where it can be ameliorated by hiring help and the like to counter the effect of a mother who has an inadequate personality. We have to ask why these people do not get out of the way when the hit-and-run drivers of this life bear down on them, why they live like a perpetual accident on its way to a happening, why a notion like "crisis intervention" becomes meaningless in a family that could not tell a crisis from its everyday life.

## Failures of Maturation

Our research began with a pilot study. This has meant "staffing" a series of cases nominated because there was, or had been, some question about the standards of child care in the household. Each case is different, of course, and there are some women who have achieved a fair level of organization and maturity. However, our outstanding impression at this time is of the relatively low level of psychogenetic development at which some of the mothers in the sample are operating.[1]

We have to ask ourselves what sort of psychiatric syndrome Hattie represents. We do not really find symptoms, since these

---

[1] I should like to express my appreciation to my colleagues Dr. John Patton, Christine DeSaix, and Mary Lou Wing, who have contributed to the clarifications in this paper.

presuppose a degree of conflict, the use of symbols, and the capacity to try to put one's troubles into a neat package. Rather, what we see is a series of troubles and miseries, of false expectations and failures to foresee, of distorted realities and lack of skills—we see, in short, not "symptoms" but manifestations of the underlying character problems. The picture is of a child at the age of an adult, who has failed to learn from the passing years. And we say that we are dealing with an immature person.

Perhaps it would be more to the point to say we are dealing with what has also been called an infantile personality. As Jurgen Ruesch pointed out in his classic paper, it is inappropriate to think of these women in terms of regression, which implies that they have fallen back from a better level of organization.[2] The truth is that we are dealing here with persons who have never advanced.

I shall not extend discussion of the various aspects of the infantile personality as they have been delineated. You are all aware of the inability to bind tension through interpersonal communication, but instead to discharge it directly, and immediately, in action and/or in somatization.

The inability to think in long-time units, to plan, to set a priority among choices, has also been noted, as has the tendency to surrender to impulses. Not so well known, perhaps, is the peculiar, rigid, all-or-nothing form taken by the superego— if it exists—and the tendency to externalize it, either because it was never properly internalized, or because it becomes such an intolerably demanding internal institution, as greedy for perfection as the client is for food. Much of this is taught in our field

[2] Jurgen Ruesch, "The Infantile Personality: The Core Problem of Psychosomatic Medicine," *Psychosomatic Medicine,* Vol. X (1948), 134–44.

through the writings of Reiner, Kaufman, and others.[3] The important thing is for us to begin to recognize that multiproblem clients are likely also to be infantile—and infantilizing. Indeed, this article might be subtitled, "Observations on the Inheritance of Immaturity."

Given that one finds the mother in a family suffers from some of these patterns, what else can one deduce? We are not in a field in which one-to-one predictions are often possible, but there are some observations I might share.

The first derives from the fact that, in marriage, people seem likely to choose partners of comparable levels of development. Indeed, when you ask one of these women how she came to choose her husband, she is likely to be at a loss for words to describe the feeling she had at the time, but the odds are that she unconsciously recognized that he operated in some way at the same level she did. It is not at all uncommon, for example, to find somewhat similar problems in middle-class women whose husbands, at first glance, seem highly intact and successful. Only gradually do we become aware that the husbands' seeming maturity and responsibility are in the service of a superego that is itself childlike; it is then we find that the somewhat disorganized woman has linked herself to a compulsive character in the mistaken belief that he will be able to provide enough adulthood for them both, along with money. While compulsive defenses may be the best we can hope for as a solution for many with problems of this order, the essential immaturity behind them is not to be overlooked. Among other things, there is the danger that if in treatment one partner begins to be freed toward growth the other will fear being left behind

[3] Beatrice S. Reiner and Irving Kaufman, *Character Disorders in Parents of Delinquents,* New York: Family Service Association of America (1959).

and abandoned.    These are problems of private practice, and of work in hospitals serving the middle class, but they are no less relevant to the treatment of the so-called multiproblem group. Hattie's husband, for example, who works as a laborer, might well have been experiencing the same explosive sense of being fed up as a dentist, an engineer, or a lawyer—not to mention a social caseworker!—with so inadequate a wife.

There is another deduction that one can make.    If the mother is as disorganized and primitive as the one depicted here, the odds are that the children will not mature much beyond her. There are a number of reasons for this, some of which must have been immediately apparent in the case illustration.    First, leaving out the process of identification that occurs at a somewhat more mature level, let us consider primitive incorporation-by-imitation.    In this home what sort of model is available from which a girl might derive an image of how to be a woman, a mother, a wife, a citizen?    Second, if development requires a shift from unconditional love to paced demands for performance, some sort of planfulness and policy-making on the part of the mother are implied.    A woman like Hattie, disorganized and living constantly in the present, seems incapable of guiding her child's maturation—or of holding to her policies, even if she could establish some.    There is also the question of how much learning about interpersonal skills can take place in a continuously unstable and impulse-ridden environment.    Finally, how would it feel to be Hattie and have a child who did "grow up."    Will Hattie feel left behind like the woman whose husband outgrows her?    Will she compete with her daughter, more as an elder sister than a mother?    Or will she push her to become her "little mother," demanding a precocious pseudo-maturity so that we will have a seven-year-old already caring for the younger children while inwardly seething, and herself never really growing beyond the age at which she was force-fed adulthood? It seems no wonder that the children of infantile personalities show such difficulties later in life. Even if they go through the primary grades as "good little boys and girls," there is always the danger that we are witnessing merely hostile compliance that breaks down rapidly in adolescence into a diffuse, disorganized rebelliousness.

It is hard for people to raise themselves by their bootstraps; it is even harder for those with a good bit of infantilism in their personalities to help their children outpace them. This is especially true when, as with so many children, there is no capacity to see limitations in themselves. It is for this reason that immaturity can be passed on from generation to generation. Sometimes it is called the "cycle of poverty"; in certain better-off families, it takes the apparent form of so-called hereditary mental illnesses since the immature rigidities and misperceptions they bring to adulthood constantly create situations leading to emotional breakdown; it invades even such public issues as conflict over civil rights, since extreme positions are being taken by immature people on both sides. Let me say, from my fairly extensive experience in private hospital work, that the only thing that prevents even more families from falling into the multiproblem category is the degree to which money can be used to buffer the children and others against the worst consequences of an inadequate or disorganized mother by purchasing the services of a matronly housekeeper, if nothing else. All concerned here may be grateful if the father's compulsiveness at least takes a form that supports his family!

## *Treatment by Interview*

There is presently much hopeful talk regarding what we can do for a broader spectrum of our clientele. I have no doubt that more can and will be done as we put more trained people

into the field and give them improved tools with which to work
But insofar as multiproblem clients represent a cadre of per
sons with the serious disorders we have termed infantile personality, let us have no illusions.  The task of bringing about
even a cessation of symptoms in a relatively well-integrated
neurotic is not an easy one.  Character alteration for anyone,
even the person who understands its necessity and offers himself
for help, is something that usually takes years in classical analysis.  Only a person accustomed to deluding himself regarding
the depth of improvement he achieves with his patients will
readily accept hopeful signs of better functioning in an infantile
character as evidence of "real growth."  It is essential to
remind ourselves, once again, that we are dealing not with persons who "once had it but lost it," but with persons whose total
personalities reflect their failure to grow up in the first place.

This immediately raises the question: How does one help
another person to mature if that person is already twenty years
of age or older?  Obviously, this is nothing one can make
happen, any more than one can press down on the ground
around one's house and bring forth shrubbery.  So far as I can
see, we can only prune away the weeds and debris that may be
impeding growth, fertilize the ground, and perhaps provide the
necessary trelliswork.  The rest is up to the plant and to nature.

As far as direct work with such clients is concerned, the task
is to become something we have been trying not to be in social
work for some time.  We must establish a relationship, encourage an entangling dependency, and act as kindly but firm educators.  This is the type of treatment recommended by all the
analysts whose work I have reason to respect, and I cannot see
how it would differ in casework.  Indeed, in the treatment of
such personality disorders, I have heard analytically trained
psychiatrists say: "I am really doing casework"—hardly aware

that their concentration on current reality, their somewhat didactic approach, their acting the Dutch uncle, was certainly not a flattering self-image of the modern-day caseworker. I trust we shall soon be far enough along to be able to assume that everybody knows casework is not just one bag of tricks, pedantically applied to every client who comes along.

Florence Hollis has recently made an excellent analytical mapping of casework processes, grouping the various techniques available under six headings. Of these, only the first three seem likely to find much applicability in direct work with infantile personalities during the early stages of treatment (which may last for several years!). These are the *sustaining procedures, procedures of direct influence,* and *catharsis or ventilation.*[4] Techniques that require the client to participate in something approaching insight therapy are inappropriate until substantial maturation has already taken place.

Indeed, it constitutes progress for the client to begin to take responsibility for his own feelings. Ruesch points out that it may be quite an advance for him to be able to say, "I hate" instead of "John Doe is nasty." [5] Such a transition already indicates that the client has begun to accept full awareness of himself as an independent entity and to risk full verbal-conceptual communication.

Nor should one anticipate that a close relationship with persons thus constituted is likely to run smoothly, what with their likelihood of being overly demanding, their direct and inflexible expression of fixed ways of dealing with others, their tendency to distort reality so as to make themselves feel better. Lewis Hill notes:

[4] Florence Hollis, *Casework: A Psychosocial Therapy,* New York: Random House (1964), pp. 71 ff.
[5] Jurgen Ruesch, "The Infantile Personality."

When infantile persons fail to get along with someone, the standard remedy may be to become ill, that is, to vomit or have diarrhea or fainting attacks. Others may regularly meet their disappointments by attacks of rage, or unclear or infantile speech, or of sulking. Among older infantile characters, the repeated technique may be that of having accidents or of resorting to alcohol or drugs. . . . The common factor in all these recurrent bits of behavior is that they let the patient feel that he has some control over things, but that none of them adds to his list of abilities and techniques for relationships to other people.[6]

Insofar as all character education must involve occasional frustration of immediate gratification, trying to help clients like these through office interviews is fraught with uneasy moments. In fact, while some may have become sufficiently concerned about psychosomatic involvement to hold themselves in treatment, it is altogether to be anticipated that a good part of the multiproblem group will break off after the first feelings of relief. All sorts of risky or self-destructive activity may go on, concurrent with (and even to spite) the casework. Should the worker survive the various storms to moments of quietude, he is likely to be met by the complaint, "But what have you done for me lately?" Social workers should know this, but do the industrialists who decided to dip into the Job Corps business *want* to know this? No, they want quick, profitable programs, even if these do not work.

I see no probability at present that any substantial portion of the very large group of infantile personalities whom we are treating will be dealt with by persons qualified to recognize their needs. Certainly, it is not going to happen in public welfare in our generation. Who will be willing to work in large bureaucracies that are unappreciative of their efforts with clients as

6 Lewis B. Hill, "Infantile Personalities," *American Journal of Psychiatry,* Vol. 109 (1952), p. 429.

difficult and exhausting as these? If they will work under such conditions, how long will they stay at the front lines? A social worker who can do a first-rate job with infantile personalities is a person sufficiently versatile to find much easier work, whenever he wants it.

Although I can see how much good can, and is, being done by direct social casework suitably adapted, it does not seem a practical solution to the challenge presented by the multiproblem client. In short, the full gamut of emotional re-education (or education) utilized among the wealthy by suitably trained and financially motivated medical therapists does not present a practical choice for social casework.

It is for this reason that I have become all the more interested in whether a concentration on the issue of verbal accessibility cannot, in itself, prove growth-enhancing for such clients.[7] It may prove a method readily transmittable to untrained workers, and there is the hope that it will release growth potentials in a goodly proportion of clients whom now we simply "keep track of," in discouraged fashion. The alternative, of course, is to accept the immature client as he is, working within the limitations of his character structure while doing what we can to protect the children involved. This is better than nothing, but it is hardly satisfactory.

## *Institutional Treatment*

We have taken into account the pervasive nature of the manifestations of personality disorders in clients from multiproblem families. One is often at a loss where to find, within

[7] See Norman A. Polansky, "The Concept of Verbal Accessibility," *Smith College Studies in Social Work,* Vol. 36, No. 1 (October 1965), pp. 1–48.

the person, a secure "peg" on which to hang the treatment process. Parts of the personality that, in more intact people, are our accomplices in the process of bringing about change are simply absent in many of these people. To talk about casework as a problem-solving process is to speak a language that is far over their heads, since they do not think of living that planfully, nor do they conceive that one can *discuss* one's way into decisions that will make one happier. By analogy, one might surmise that large-scale personality alteration might require a therapeutic immersion far beyond the office interview.

I have no doubt that the excellent homemaker services now being encouraged by the United States Children's Bureau were conceived with something like this in mind.[8] I suppose it would be impolitic to push them with the full rationale I am stating here. But there is no doubt that, with many of these mothers, one's better chance of bringing about change is to rely on quite childlike mechanisms of concrete behavior rather than to try to teach through verbal communication, at least during the earlier phases of contact. My question, however, is whether homemaker services try to move to the verbal level of treatment, once a certain amount of early integration has been achieved in these women—or if the homemaker service is offered with its rationale thought through this far at all.

A solution that should be given more consideration would be the use of inpatient treatment for more of these clients. I have in mind particularly the mothers, despite the difficulty in sparing them, because they make such a difference in the next generation. In fact, institutional care may well be the treatment of choice for a good many people, and it might be better for it to be undertaken sooner than later. I say this because a goodly

[8] *Homemaker Service: How it Helps Children.* Washington, D.C.: Children's Bureau Publication Number 443, 1967 (pamphlet).

proportion of severe neurotic reactions and psychotic break-downs occur in persons whose character structure is so primitive, and so limits their adaptability, that they constantly work themselves into situations they themselves describe as "traps." As anxiety rises and their tension becomes unbearable (they never had too much frustration tolerance, anyway), they find it necessary to take leave of reality. Hence, it is a consistent experience in inpatient psychiatric treatment that, even after the more severe symptoms subside, one may still be left with the manifestations of an immature personality that, left untreated, can only guarantee further trouble for the patient.

The idea of institutional treatment for such clients is not new, but in my own experience it is unlikely to be offered in this country unless there is a fair amount of discomfort and/or the client becomes addicted—and is well-off financially. However, I must remind you that Maxwell Jones's famous therapeutic community was originally devised for a patient population very much like this one.[9]

There are a number of advantages to inpatient treatment for such clients. Because of their impulsivity, it may be impossible for the caseworker to get clients to stay out of difficulties long enough to take any sort of look at the long-range pattern they are expressing. Life is one emergency after another, provoked as often as blundered into. Hence, one yearns for a controlled environment in which inhibitions might be supported long enough for energy to find more acceptable modes of expression. Second, an inpatient setting can provide a wide variety of auxiliary services to hasten and intensify the processes of education and re-education. These may include everything from art and social dancing to group therapy and psychodrama—the

[9] Maxwell Jones, *The Therapeutic Community,* New York: Basic Books (1964).

latter being a milieu in which the client can begin to differen-
tiate other people's reactions from his own, and begin to acquire
some interpersonal skills.   Third, working with very immature
clients in the community operates against the constant threat
that they will break treatment prematurely if one crosses them,
something less likely to happen once they have attached themselves to an inpatient setting.   Finally, insofar as it may become
necessary, one can, in a hospital or other whole-life situation,
deal with clients at the concrete level that may be required—
"Since you did that again, you will not get to do such and such
for three days."

Unfortunately, such inpatient treatment is not going to be
practical for very many cases.   But impracticality is no justification for refusing to recognize what is the treatment of choice.
This is despite the fact that, as with any other intervention,
institutional treatment can have its noxious side effects, some of
which are to be carefully guarded against, if possible.

At present such total-life help usually cannot be offered to a
mother unless she has the forethought to offer us a mental
breakdown.   In Washington, D. C., there is an experimental
program in which young mothers are admitted to live in a con-
gregate building for six months or more, bringing with them
their whole families.   Such an arrangement offers an opportunity
to try to "get at" the mother in a variety of ways, while teaching
her skills ranging from homemaking and personal hygiene to
child care and work habits.[10]   The mothers cared for in this
unusual program are not all to be characterized as infantile
personalities, of course, but does it not seem likely that it would

[10] *Toward Social and Economic Independence: The First Three Years
of the District of Columbia Training Center.*   Department of Public
Welfare, Washington, D.C., June 1965 (pamphlet).

require a program as bold as this to reach some multiproblem cases?

Related to this is a movement about which I used to hear, and of which I wish I were now hearing more. This is "family camping," motivated by the good intention of giving mothers a chance at a vacation even if they are poor and have many children. One cannot expect miracles out of a two- or four-week experience, but I imagine that something like this arrangement might be the way to progress for some of the families we are discussing. (With some of the multiproblem cases, just getting them packed to leave for one place, all at the same time, might already indicate more maturation than the family camping could ever provide!)

I dwell on institutional treatment because I am aware that the big movement in our field is away from the institution, both in child welfare and in psychiatric illness. In our enthusiasm to abolish this usually unsightly blemish on the corpus of mental health in the United States, we must not forget the positive values that can accrue from a properly conducted inpatient effort. The only mothers in multiproblem families now receiving the better quality of this type of care are those for whom one of the multiple problems has not been the father's incapacity to keep making money. Maybe something should be said for the compulsive personality, if only as a purchaser of treatment for everyone but himself!

### Conclusion

The changing direction in treatment of the multiproblem client has primarily been toward offering improved opportunities of various kinds. A substantial proportion of such clients are to be understood most clearly as instances of arrested psychogenetic development, adults trying to cope with adult problems with part of their mental and emotional equipment still grossly immature. They will not usually take advantage of the opportunities offered. Sooner or later a confrontation of the treatment problems present in such cases is going to require sober evaluation of the limited level on which they are able to operate.

Such an evaluation does not encourage a sanguine expectation about rates of success, or about minimal cost of treatment. To do what nature has not originally done is tedious, difficult, and expensive. However, a good deal is known about how to deal with these cases. Depending on the level of development represented by a specific client, treatment may range from modified office-interview strategies to total inpatient effort. The big thing is that caseworkers must not become rigidified in their conceptions of "what a caseworker does," or of what is conceivably necessary treatment. Such limitations would mean trying to meet the needs of the infantile personality with a similarly stereotyped and limited infantile discipline

# Advocacy and Political Behavior *

## GEORGE A. BRAGER

SOCIAL WORK'S QUEST for new techniques is a response to the social climate. The dynamism of the times has resulted in dissatisfaction with such concepts as worker neutrality or adherence to enabling as a major tenet of method.[1] Agencies that assist the poor to participate in community activities cannot, with equanimity, proclaim their neutrality when controversial issues are engaged. The contradiction of a community agency able and willing to help residents challenge community conditions, but unable or unwilling to put itself "on the line" as well is not lost on its constituency.[2] In the face of passion, neutrality seems like timidity and enabling seems unresponsive.

* This article first appeared in *Social Work,* Vol. 13, No. 2, April 1968.

[1] Rothman defines the enabling role as "providing an accepting and facilitating social climate and procedural means through which individuals are encouraged to think their problems through and make valid decisions from their own internal resources. . . . The parallel to Rogerian nondirective psychotherapy with individuals is obvious." Jack Rothman, "An Analysis of Goals and Roles in Community Organization Practice," *Social Work,* Vol. 9, No. 2 (April 1964), pp. 26 and 27.

[2] Examples from work with individuals are available as well. Although enabling and nondirectiveness are not synonymous, they have a natural affinity, and in practice are associated with one another. In such cases, a client might be expected to respond as follows: "Miss K., the social worker, gave us a letter to take to Welfare. If she had gone with us instead, it would have been different. . . . She's very nice, Miss K., but I don't know what she's going to do for me. She looks at me, smiles, and says, 'Hm-um, hm-um!' Well, life just isn't that calm for us." George Brager and Sherman Barr, "Perceptions and Reality: The Poor Man's View of Social Agencies," in Brager and Francis Purcell, *Community Action Against Poverty,* New Haven: College and University Press (1967), p. 79.

Methodological questioning has also been furthered by the infusion of social science knowledge into the field of social work. Of particular significance in this regard is the increased understanding of the contextual aspects of events. Attitudes develop, behavior is shaped, interactions take place, and incidents occur in response to current structural arrangements, not merely as reflections of the psychological patterns of individual actors or their past environmental conditions.

These currents impel, in their turn, a consideration of the role of the social worker as advocate.[3] Although the concept is both important and in current use, its methodological implications have not yet been seriously considered. The worker as advocate identifies with the plight of the disadvantaged. He sees as his primary responsibility the tough-minded and partisan representation of their interests, and this supersedes his fealty to others. This role inevitably requires that the practitioner function as a political tactician. It is this aspect of advocacy with which this paper deals.

## Redistribution of Power

The context in which change is espoused, clients are helped to achieve it, or are taught how to work effectively for desired social ends must be taken into account. When this is done, one turns inevitably to the making of the community's agenda. Who defines the problems that need remedy? Or their causation and solutions? As has been noted elsewhere:

The groups that are feeling the impact of "bad" social conditions frequently lack the strength or voice to be heard. Such groups as the victims of poverty, neglected children, unemployed youth, mi-

---

[3] The concept of advocacy as a professional strategy was introduced into the social work literature by Charles Grosser in "Community Development Programs Serving the Urban Poor," *Social Work*, Vol. 10 No. 3 (July 1965), pp. 15–21.

grants, the uneducated, the victims of discrimination, and the aging cannot compete easily in the market of ideas and vested interests.[4]

These groups are also the least likely to be involved in community decision-making processes or, when involved, to be influential participants. One of the advocate's objectives may be conceptualized as the redistribution of community power so that programs and policies that benefit the disadvantaged may receive more vigorous and receptive attention. This does not mean, of course, that low-income persons or groups have a lien on either virtue or wisdom. It means, rather, that in a pluralistic and democratic society disproportionate differentials in influence must be adjusted.

The social worker, himself hardly a powerful figure in our society, is not in a commanding position. His authority is weak and the resources at his disposal that would influence the community decision-making process are sharply circumscribed. Fear of abusing his professional power through its untrammeled application is, in this context, unrelated to reality—although to believe otherwise may be irresistibly appealing to his professional self-image. For the social worker in his role as a model to eschew political behavior or to counsel his clients or constituents to avoid it, even indirectly, is to diminish still further the ability of the disadvantaged and their professional advocates to influence community change. Professional purity is likely to be most costly to the victims of social problems.

*Violating Principles*

The social agency—the worker's own and his colleagues'—must also be seen as part of the worker's field of forces. Social

[4] Nathan E. Cohen, "A Social Work Approach," in Cohen, ed., *Social Work and Social Problems,* New York: National Association of Social Workers (1964), p. 374.

work is a profession practiced largely from an agency base, and yet it is only recently that organizational requisites have begun to receive attention.[5]   The agency provides the workers with both opportunities and constraints, but what counsel is there for maximizing the former and minimizing the latter?

Social workers have perhaps been unduly simplistic; they have advised their fellow workers that they have a responsibility to influence changes in policies with which they disagree but have not specified the professionally acceptable and effective means of doing so.   They have suggested that if agency policy violates principle and cannot be influenced to change, the professional may—and sometimes should—leave.   But this leaves the clients in the lurch and the violated principle intact.   Furthermore, to counsel such a course ignores the manifold influences on the worker, one of which is his need for a job.

The fact is that all organizations violate principles at one time or another.   Agencies can be ranged on a continuum as to their amenability to influence and their violation of practice norms, yet this has not really been considered.   Is the same advice offered to the welfare department employee, the social worker in the public schools, the neighborhood center group worker, and the psychiatric caseworker in the family agency? And, if so, are workers not being implicitly encouraged to seek employment in the small voluntary agency, in which professional norms tend to be observed and professional influence is greatest?

If social workers believe that agencies are dedicated to client

[5] See, for example, George Brager, "Institutional Change: Perimeters of the Possible," *Social Work,* Vol. 12, No. 1 (January 1967), pp. 59–69; Martin Rein and Robert Morris, "Goals, Structures and Strategies for Community Change," *Social Work Practice, 1962,* New York: Columbia University Press (1962), pp. 127–45; Mayer N. Zald, "Organizations As Polities: An Analysis of Community Organization Agencies," *Social Work,* Vol. 11, No. 4 (October 1966), pp. 56–65.

interests, they face little conflict between their organizational and professional responsibilities. If they believe that agencies are sufficiently interested in their clients' welfare to respond to a reasoned appeal for policy change, they successfully avoid the issue. But what if they are convinced that the maintenance and enhancement needs of organizations take precedence over clients' needs, even in the best of agencies? Or that conflict between the needs of the organization and the needs of its constituents is inevitable? This is likely to be the advocate's perception, since his single-minded focus on the client will make him most sensitive to unmet needs and to policies that act to the detriment of clients.

To whom, then, is the worker's primary responsibility: the agency or the client? If the former, the issue is simply met. If the latter—as in the case of the advocate—the agency may well become a target for change. The worker who has thus opted in favor of his clients' interests is likely to feel he owes it to them to be as effective as possible. Considering the structure of influence in the social agency, his own potency as a member of the staff group—not to mention his clients' or constituencies' power—is likely to be limited. To be effective, he may have to use political strategies. To avoid them on the grounds of professional purity may once again be most costly to the victims of social problems.

## *Ingroup Defenses*

And all of this is likely to apply equally or more in the advocate's dealing with colleagues and their agencies. All professions develop self-protective mechanisms, shielding their members from outside criticism or intrusion. Thus the doctor, for example, does not reveal what he has observed in the operating room, and thereby protects his colleagues from lay scrutiny. Similarly, a study of the public schools reports the perception of teachers that one of the principal's major functions is to protect them from faultfinding by parents.[6] The norms are understandable. Commonness of experience and shared interests lead inevitably to ingroup defenses. It may also be that the norms make it possible for the system to function smoothly, by keeping each actor aware of the support he may expect from the others.

To sanctify norms as professional ethics is another matter, and to deny their self-serving nature would be untoward in a field that emphasizes self-knowledge and understanding. The worker who is strongly client-identified will be aware of this, especially since much of his work entails helping clients to negotiate with workers in massive service systems. In dealing with his colleagues he may or may not appear to observe the norms, but he will surely violate them in fact.

Organizations also are circumspect in their relationships with one another; one social agency is responsive to the interests of another. Social work literature is replete with references to the advantages of co-ordination among agencies, with little attention given to the disadvantages. This is not meant to challenge interagency co-ordination, but to note that the concept of co-ordination may be used by agencies to protect their "turf." Devising geographic boundaries as a basis for service does, after all, insure that agencies will not compete for clientele.

It is curious that a nation devoted to free enterprise and competition does not hold these values for its service agencies. Yet the principle is the same. If clients could choose from among a number of welfare agencies, it is likely that the service

[6] Howard S. Becker, "The Teacher in the Authority System of the Public School," in Amitai Etzioni, ed., *Complex Organizations: A Sociological Reader,* New York: Holt, Rinehart & Winston (1961), pp. 243–51.

at all these agencies would be better than it is. Co-ordination may be more beneficial to the serving agencies than to the served.[7]

Norms that regulate interorganizational relationships also pose issues for the advocate social worker; his focus on clients' needs may threaten to impair his agency's relationship with other important organizations. He must then walk the tightrope between conflicting demands. If client identification is uppermost to him, he will present the case to his agency in a way most likely to garner support for a client-oriented course of action. This may require that he minimize the risk to his agency while underscoring the importance of his client's interests. He may even argue the case with more passion than he feels, if he believes that his emotional tone will positively affect his gaining administrative support. He will, in short, engage in political behavior.

## *Political Behavior*

What is meant by political behavior? It must be clear so far in this paper that it does *not* mean a relation to government or skill in governing. The term does, however, encompass many other meanings. The dictionaries include the following as synonyms for "politic": artful, shrewd, crafty, expedient, and prudent. In order to sharpen the inquiry into the advocate's technology, one aspect of "artfulness" will be emphasized—the conscious rearranging of reality to induce a desired attitudinal or behavioral outcome.

Reality may be arranged with the knowledge of those affected, as when social workers artificially create interracial groups and explain their interest in changing interracial atti-

[7] This idea was suggested to the author by Professor Irving Miller of the Columbia University School of Social Work, New York, New York.

tudes, or it may be rearranged without their knowledge, as when the groups are created without giving an interpretation. There is also the gray area, in which reality is not arranged but information is withheld, as when a worker does not share a perception with a client because he believes the client is not "ready" for it or when a student is led by his supervisor's questions to an answer the supervisor knew all the time.[8]

Generally, the values of social workers allow reality rearrangements when the fact is shared with those affected although even here questions of values can be raised. It is when the arrangements are secret or ill defined that negative prescriptions are invoked and the action is called "manipulative." It is the argument of this paper that in the context in which social workers function, advocacy requires political behavior, and political behavior includes manipulation.

In recent years, Richard Christie and other social psychologists have conducted intensive studies of manipulation. A scale has been developed by culling from Machiavelli's writings those statements that appear to have relevance to the ways in which people view one another or to their means of controlling or influencing the behavior of others. The scale, intended to measure the respondent's acceptance of manipulation or the use of guile in interpersonal relations, appears to have predictive validity; academicians who were identified by their colleagues as "smooth operators" scored higher than others.[9] In laboratory

[8] These examples are not offered with the intent of being judgmental but I cannot resist the comment that the technique of leading a student to a predetermined answer by questioning, although a common pedagogical device, is basically dishonest. It is better for the supervisor to express an opinion and to follow it by questions in a climate that encourages students to challenge the supervisor's ideas.

[9] Richard Christie, "The Prevalence of Machiavellian Orientations," paper presented at the annual meeting of the American Psychological Association, Los Angeles, September 1964. (Mimeographed.)

experiments involving a series of three-person games, those who scored high on the scale were consistently and dramatically the victors.[10]

Unfortunately, there have been no samples of social workers in these experiments. Although a related professional group— the social psychologists—score consistently high as a group, the studies done of the medical profession are most interesting. Physicians' scores vary depending on their medical specialization. They are as follows in descending order: psychiatry, pediatrics, internal medicine, obstetrics, and surgery.[11] This finding is reported, not to indicate that psychiatrists are less moral or principled than their fellow physicians or the rest of us, but to point up Christie's interpretation that the degree of interpersonal manipulation required by a person's formal role (or job) is the most salient factor in explaining his response to the scale. Persons oriented to social roles that involve influencing others, he notes, are more in agreement with Machiavelli than are persons who are oriented primarily to the manipulation of things or pure ideas.[12] The point, of course, is not that artfulness is necessarily desirable, but that it is an inevitable concomitant of certain roles and tasks.

## *Three Professional Approaches*

This finding may profitably be applied to social work. There are three general professional approaches, each fashioned by its objectives: the process orientation, the clinical, and the social reform.

[10] Florence Geis, "Machiavellianism and the Manipulation of One's Fellow Man," paper presented at the annual meeting of the American Psychological Association, Los Angeles, September 1964. (Mimeographed.)
[11] Christie, "The Prevalence of Machiavellian Orientations," pp. 12–13.
[12] *Ibid.,* p. 14.

*Process orientation.* Although the terminology is loose because all approaches in social work are concerned with process, the process orientation is distinct from the others in that process is valued for its own sake. The professional facilitates and guides the interaction among persons or mediates between persons and institutional officials without his own preconceived notions about desired outcomes. Goals are set by the participants and the professional's task is to insure that issues are effectively confronted.

Assuming that professional practice without goals is possible, the process-oriented worker is likely to be less manipulative than others.[13] Ideally, he is neutral; with no stake in the outcome, he feels little pressure to influence the attitudes or behavior of others and, therefore, less need for artfulness as it has been defined previously. But although he is freer of value conflict than his colleagues, he is probably also less effective in dealing with behavioral change or significant issues.

Process orientation ignores context. It assumes, for example, that communication itself may solve problems, without sufficient regard for the circumstances in which the communication takes place or the differentials in influence among the communicators. The worker who initiates a process between tenants and public housing officials without, in practice, accounting for the differences in power between the parties is hardly likely to affect public housing arrangements. He may even run the risk of being defined as a "cop out" by the tenants and a "do-gooder" by the officials.

[13] The author does not, in fact, make the assumption that professional practice without goals is possible. Quite the contrary; he believes that goal-less practice is not possible, and that its proponents have a difficult time making a case for it. They say, for example, that workers have "purposes" but not goals. But this is outside the scope of the current discussion.

*Clinical orientation.* A second approach to social work may be referred to broadly as a clinical or treatment orientation. The professional seeks improved functioning of his clients— changes in their personality, attitudes, or behavior. Although the client seeks the help and the changes are ultimately his own, the professional assumes responsibility for diagnosing the problem and "prescribing" the treatment. The social worker does, of course, have ends in mind and a stake in the outcome. For these reasons, and because he attempts, as does the psychiatrist, to influence others, he is likely to engage in manipulative activity. If Christie is correct, the formal role of the clinician makes this inevitable.

The field's negative prescriptions may thus be problematic, since they encourage or require the denial of guileful behavior and this makes its proper examination impossible. Its inevitability cannot be explored without emotional overtones, nor can consideration be made of whether there are circumstances in which artfulness is professionally justified or appropriate, what those circumstances are, in regard to whom, and within what limits.

*Social reform.* The objective of the third approach is reform. It seeks to make an impact on social problems by influencing change in organizations and institutions. Although advocacy *may* be found in any professional interaction in which a client's interest is opposed by some other person or institution, it *must* be a part of the worker's armamentarium when environmental change is the objective. The necessity for political-manipulative behavior by the advocate has already been argued; it need only be added that the reformer is more likely to embrace this activity than are his professional colleagues with different orientations. There are at least two reasons for this in addition to those referred to earlier.

Collectivities that press for change will try to make the most effective case for their position rather than the most complete or reasoned one. They will scale their demands for change to strategic considerations, asking for more than is achievable or less than they need, depending on what is deemed tactical. They will be concerned as much with their appearance of strength or influence as with the reality, since the two are related. They will, in short, engage in politics. The advocate-reformer is likely to be at least as interested in the specific change pursued by these groups as they are and may even be more so. He will therefore join them in the manipulative activity.

Furthermore, the advocate-reformer is less likely than other social workers to be concerned with a role of authority or the imposition of his beliefs. Imposition and manipulation do, of course, entail different behaviors and are to some extent opposed to one another. A worker who is overbearing may impose his point of view, but this is not being manipulative. On the other hand, successful manipulation necessarily involves imposition. The client's choice is bent to the worker's desire if the worker distorts information or if environmental conditions are arranged to induce the outcome to which the worker aspires. In any case, the power relations between clients and social workers are likely to be quite different, depending on the context of their relationship.

Clients are dependent on the professional when they are engaged in an intense treatment relationship. On the other hand, the worker who needs constituent support for a social action effort is the seeker in the relationship and, consequently, wields less authority. In petitioning for community change, he is again the suppliant and his influence is often considerably less than that of the officialdom with which he deals. Lesser authority and power—in combination with client identification and social change commitment—are likely to foster in the social worker a belief in both the necessity and the justification of employing political strategies. There is, therefore, less need to deny the professional relevance of these methods.

If manipulation is inevitable for the professional who attempts to influence others or is justified by particular objectives or a specific context, one must address the issues thus posed. For it could hardly be proposed that there be a moratorium on morality or suggested that "anything goes." Rather, it is necessary for professional guidelines to be imposed on the use of political methods. One set of rules is needed having to do with values; another, with effectiveness or expediency (although at times the two do merge).

### Who Benefits, Who Loses?

To make value judgments one must assess situations on an individual basis, taking a number of factors into account. Although it is not possible to establish rigid rules, broad standards may nevertheless be developed, relating to (1) who benefits and who loses, (2) the subject of the political activity, (3) the principle involved or the end pursued, and (4) the nature of the political act.

Professional ideals require that the end of political behavior must not be the interest of the professional himself. Although, unconsciously or otherwise, this rule may be breached in the reality, such behavior should not be encouraged or condoned, especially when it might conflict with the client's needs. The justification for violation of any cherished value must be its inherent conflict with some other value of equal or greater import. It follows, then, that manipulation should generally be eschewed except when it is clearly in the best interests of the disadvantaged client. The magnitude of the need, the power-lessness of the client, and the rules of the game as played by his adversaries dictate the conclusion that manipulation is some-times justified. This is at the other end of the continuum from using it to further the professional's self-interest. Falling midway between the two are the interests of one's agency and other clients or constituents.

Certain cautions must be introduced before artfulness may be counseled comfortably, even in the "best interests" of the client. One has to do with risk. For example, a strategy might be pursued that is in the long-term interest of the client but that risks losses to him in the short run. (Some advocates' fervor for change makes this a ready possibility.) Thus, an advocate of the rent strike as a tactic for housing improvement may try to convince tenants to withhold their rent no matter what the cost. On the other hand, if he understands the risks to the tenants, he will avoid both imposition and manipulation; instead he will try to make clear to them what their choices are and the dangers that might be involved, however much this approach might inhibit the success of the effort.

Social workers working in a labor union setting recently found themselves in a situation like this. Union officials favored creating an incident that would force an eviction so that the attendant uproar would attract attention to the problem. In this instance the social workers' advocacy led them to insist that no eviction be promoted without the understanding and con-currence of the tenants and the union's assurance of support.

The worker's wish to serve the best interests of his client is a necessary but not a sufficient condition to justify manipulation.

Good intentions have been used, sincerely and otherwise, to excuse base actions. To arrange events or shape information in order to control another's action may be inevitable, but it should not be professionally approved unless other factors are also considered, such as the importance of the issue involved and the object of the manipulation.

## Objects of Political Behavior

Considering the possible objects of an advocate's political behavior raises a complex question, especially in community organization, in which there is confusion as to who the client is. To say that the community is the organizer's client is to deal in an abstraction that has scant meaning. "Community" is too broad a term to have a discernible empirical referent. One may more profitably conceptualize the organizer's (and other advocates') relations to three systems: client, action, and target.

*Client system.* The term "client" usually refers to one who engages the services of a professional and, in this sense, social workers do not ordinarily have clients. In social work usage the term connotes those whose interests are served. This has been taken to mean persons in interaction with a professional. In community organization, however, until quite recently direct contact has been with the providers, rather than the recipients, of service and this remains a significant component of community organization practice. Defining the client system to mean those who benefit or are intended to benefit from the worker's activity alters one's professional perspective. Prescriptions are different when the beneficiaries of a committee's process and, therefore, the primary concern for the professional, are not the participants. His activity may be appropriately evaluated by how well he represents the absent client rather than by how well he serves the member in attendance.

*Action system.*   The action system may be viewed as composed of those who are engaged in the planned action, e.g., the committee mentioned previously.   Other examples would be the worker, client, and perhaps the worker's agency in cases of individual advocacy when intercession is necessary with another service system.   Client and action systems overlap when the benficiaries and those who are actually involved in the planned action are the same, as when groups of the poor organize to affect service systems in which they are recipients.

*Target systems.*   Target systems are those groups, programs, or institutions that are strategic to the change attempt and that need to be modified if the objective of the process is to be attained.   A school system, welfare department, or housing authority might constitute a target for change.   In such instances interaction between the professional and the target system might or might not take place.

This prescription would permit worker politicking in descending scale from target systems to action and then client systems. Four considerations guide this viewpoint: (1) the similarity of objectives between the advocate and others, (2) the quality of their interaction, (3) their relative influence, and (4) the rules by which the game is played.

When there are both similarity of objectives and interaction that permits shared understanding, as is the case with professionals in their dealings with most clients and many action systems, manipulative behavior violates a trust.   On the other hand, as disparity of influence widens between the parties, guile becomes more understandable and more justifiable.   In this view, a dependent client's manipulation of a worker is more understandable than is a professional's manipulation of the client. And if the structure of an action group is such that it inhibits or forecloses decision-making by client groups, political activity may be the only appropriate professional response.

Furthermore, as advocacy is accepted as an appropriate strategy, social workers become increasingly involved in arenas broader than social services. To play by one's own rules without cognizance of others' rules may be to suffer irreparable disadvantage (although again, perhaps, only to the clients).

One sharp illustration would be when a government official lies in his dealings with social workers. For example, when Mobilization For Youth, the Lower East Side's (New York City) delinquency prevention and antipoverty project, was under attack for "agitating the community," it was discovered that New York City's deputy mayor was feeding false information to the press. When confronted by agency officials with his press quotations, the deputy mayor categorically denied, contrary to all evidence, that he had made the statements. It could hardly be expected, for value reasons at any rate, that agency officials would feel bound to be utterly truthful in their dealings with him.

A third important standard in evaluating the appropriateness of political strategies relates to the values inherent in the substantive end or principle at issue. Risks to life and limb, basic needs, and social justice are areas that justify political intervention. Manipulation by or on behalf of the victims of discrimination in a case of clear social injustice would thus be appropriate, e.g., in response to the jailing of civil rights workers. Similarly, one could condone a lie to entice a potential suicide off a ledge, although one would be highly critical of such behavior in other instances.

*Image Management*

Moreover, there is the nature of the act itself. One important aspect of political skill is image management. It takes many forms and is engaged in by almost everyone.[14] It is a feature of organizations as well as of people. Banfield, for example, in a study of civic associations in Chicago, describes a technique:

A common, indeed almost invariable, feature of the process by which an issue is prepared for settlement is a ceremonial appeal to the authority of "objective facts." . . . although the issue must . . . always be settled on grounds that are political in the broad sense, and although crucial judgments that are involved . . . cannot possibly be made in a purely . . . technical way, nevertheless the almost unvarying practice is to make it appear that the decision rests upon "objective" and even "factual" grounds. . . . This extraordinary devotion to "facts" is often associated with an extraordinary determination to conceal what is really at issue. . . .[15]

Images may be fabricated in a number of ways. One may withhold information or exaggerate, distort, or lie. The supervisor who counsels a graduate student worker not to indicate his student status to a client is guilty of the first; undue expressions of psychological support to clients on scanty bases are examples of the second. These may be professional errors, but they do not violate professional sensibilities. The point is that manipulative actions are of different orders of morality. In the present view, the appropriateness of a guileful act must be evaluated by the act itself in combination with the other standards that have been suggested. It is the balancing of these factors in the particular instance that determines the morality.

[14] For a cogent and diverting exposition of this viewpoint, see Erving Goffman, *The Presentation of Self in Everyday Life,* New York: Doubleday & Co. (1959).

[15] Edward C. Banfield, *Political Influence,* New York: Free Press of Glencoe (1961), p. 183.

Moral relativism is an uncomfortable thing. Fortunately, professional choices are limited by factors of effectiveness or expediency as well as by one's value framework. Although the latter has been a major focus of this paper, it is not so distinct from pragmatic concerns as may have been implied.

There are those who maintain that manipulation is self-defeating in the long run. They do not explain, however, the prevalence of this self-defeating behavior. And they would undoubtedly find it difficult to account for the results of the experiments cited earlier or for such findings that show that male students, controlled for ability, score higher on the Machiavelli scale and get better grades in the universities.[16]

Political behavior requires the same sensitivity to oneself and others as is required in all human interaction. It may even require more. Manipulation is neither self-defeating nor effective. The potential costs of political strategies must always be assessed against their potential gains, so that one's morality is supported by expedience. Social workers may use up their currency as, for example, when a person develops a reputation for guile. With his motives suspect, his hidden agendas revealed to view, and his word in doubt, he can hardly be an effective advocate. Since people resent being treated as means to an end rather than as ends in themselves, those who appear to use them instrumentally are likely to be ineffective.

Different individuals and groups are differentially tolerant of being the target of political activity and will evaluate the experience differently. The value prescriptions mentioned earlier are also relevant in this regard. People are likely to be more charitable toward guile exercised in behalf of disadvantaged clients concerning a significant issue than toward guile exercised

[16] Jerome E. Singer, "The Use of Manipulative Strategies: Machiavellianism and Attractiveness," *Sociometry*, Vol. 27, No. 2 (June 1964), pp. 128–50. Ability was measured by the admissions test battery.

in a professional's self-interest or concerning a matter of small moment. Most significantly, perhaps, the nature of the relationship or situation creates an expectation that either minimizes or maximizes the consequences of political behavior. Three such may be cited.

*Adversary situations.* In adversary situations there is considerable margin for political behavior; both parties ordinarily expect it, and discovery would cause little further disruption. Thus, target systems, for example, become ready candidates. The welfare worker whom the advocate is flattering, cajoling, disputing, intimidating, or threatening in behalf of his client questions the advocate's information, quietly makes assessments of his strength, and would not be shocked by the suggestion that he was lacking in candor.

*Differences of interest.* Situations short of conflict, in which there are differences of interest clear to both parties, allow a smaller margin of safety. The prospective employer hardly expects complete openness from the job applicant. The professor is likely to expect to be, in some measure, "conned" by the student. The conning becomes problematic only when it is stupidly or grossly done, is the student's predominant way of relating, or takes place after a significant relationship has developed.

*Ongoing relationships.* In an ongoing relationship or process the dangers of manipulation are significant. For here trust is expected between the parties and discovery may be seriously damaging to the attainment of immediately desired objectives and, more important, to the long-range relationship. In part, a determination of strategy depends on an evaluation of the importance of the present instance as compared with future need. One might not distort the truth to the potential suicide teetering on the ledge if one were his worker, anticipated a continued treatment relationship with him, and could conceive of any alternative method of deterring him. Manipulation in an ongoing relationship, which contravenes the rules understood by both parties, is not only of dubious morality but fraught with risk.

## Conclusion

There is, of course, risk in any case. Professionals function at the fulcrum of a field of interacting interest—agency board and executive, supervisor, those who are supervised, clients, community groups, government officials, and the like. Treading the path through the varying expectations, values, and demands of these disparate groups requires risk-taking and a high order of political skill. It is the author's argument that the advocate—the professional who identifies with the victims of social problems and who pursues modification in social conditions—will need to have the professional dedication to take the risk and to be political.

# Index

Addams, Jane, 18, 38

Administration: need for development as an art and skill, 6-7, 14, 16-17

Advocacy: of institutions, 45-46; of indigenous workers, 47-48; of social workers, 102-7, 111-13, 114, 117, 121

Aged, *see* Old age

Aid to Families With Dependent Children, 8, 83

Alinsky, Saul, 46

American Medical Association, 24

Antipoverty (Great Society) Program, 7, 28, 40, 43

Appalachia and Appalachian Highlanders, 61, 63-65, 71; rural multiproblem family in, case study, 82-87

Atlanta, Georgia, 42

Banfield, Edward C.: quoted, 118

Beck, Duane W.: paper by, 37-54

Bernstein, Basil, 73-74

Beveridge, Lord William: quoted, 15

Beveridge report, 4

Big Brothers, 77

Brager, George A.: paper by, 101-21

British Association for the Advancement of Science, 73

Canada, 6, 8, 10

Caplan, Gerald, 39

Chicago, Ill., 118

Children: allowances, 7, 52; Aid to families with Dependent Children, 8, 83; services for, 10; care, 48; deprived, 56, 57-58, 60-61; illegitimate, 57; Spanish-American, 72-73; parent-child relationship, 86-87, 90-91, 98-99

Christie, Richard, 108, 109, 111

Citizens' Advice Bureaus, 44

Client(s), 14-15; eligibility, 13-14; class structure and status, 20, 24; changing, relation to services, 22-36; as human beings, 38-40; hoplessness of, 46, 68; deprived, 68, 71, 73-76; multiproblem, changing concepts in treatment, 81-100; with personality disorders, treatment of, 91-99; definition, 115

Client-worker relationship, 29, 34, 47, 48, 106, 108; changes in services, 22-36; deprived individuals, 74-76; treatment in multiproblem cases, 81-100; social worker as advocate for, 102-7, 111-13, 114; professional approaches, 109-13; system, 115-16; *see also* Social worker

Cohen, Nathan E., 33; quoted, 102-3

Colorado Medical School, 31

Community: relation of social work to, 18, 31-32, 40; changes through social work, 39-41, 101

Community planning, 76-78, 102-3

Community services and programs, 18, 19, 51, 115; changes in social work concepts in treatment and prevention of problems, 37-54; information and referral programs, 43-46; criticisms of, 46-48; nonprofessional (indigenous) employees in, 47-48; mental health centers, 48-49; for de-